Book P1

How to Tell the World About Your Book

(Even if you're not on Facebook yet)

From the owner of Bravado Publishing

"This book is your map to the land of bestseller status. It's complete with the best shortcuts."
—Paul Godines, Adapt on a Dime.

"Over the years I've seen many fine books written that failed to find their readership. ***Book Promoting 101*** overflows with practical and contemporary information regarding how to get the finished book into the hands of readers -- lots of readers. Want to create a sound strategy for selling your book? ***Book Promoting 101*** provides a great road map."
—Karen Tolley, Bookseller

© 2011 Kristen James
Published by Bravado Publishing
www.bravadopublishing.com

www.bookpromoting101.com
A blog all about book promoting.

First Edition

ISBN 978-0-9846368-2-2

Library of Congress Control Number: 2010919366

Visit the author's website at
www.writerkristenjames.com
kristen@writerkristenjames.com

Also By Kristen Bailey (Kristen James):

The River People
Young Adult Native American Fiction

The Enemy's Son, published by Lachesis Publishing
A Romantic Suspense Novel

A Cowboy For Christmas
A Contemporary Romance

Acknowledgements

Thanks to

Author B. K. Mayo for writing an article, "Marketing Books Through Fundraisers for Nonprofits," for this book, sharing information and ideas on promotion and offering valuable feedback on this and other projects.

Poet Joe Federico for his thoughtful review and comments for improving this book.

Joanna Penn for allowing me to use her book marketing plan as an example in this book and providing readers at large a wealth of information on her blog, www.thecreativepenn.com.

Stephen Blake Mettee for permission to reprint his article "Getting Your Book to the Tipping Point."

Bob Baker for his article "The 7 Attributes of Highly Successful Authors."

And editor Wendell Anderson.

Highlighted Table of Contents

Part 1: Promoting While Writing
PAGE 11

Part 2: Promoting Before You Publish
PAGE 51

Part 3: Your Book Launch
PAGE 78

Part 4: The New Publishing World
PAGE 125

Part 5: Success Stories and Resources
PAGE 131

Index
PAGE 140

Detailed Table of Contents

About This Book

Book Promoting 101 is all about educating authors so they can succeed.

I began writing at a young age and subscribed to *Writer's Digest* magazine before high school. I sent out a manuscript for the first time during my freshman year, and since then, I have studied everything I could about writing and the publishing industry. Now I'm a published author and editor, and I own and operate Bravado Publishing.

Through my work, I've met authors who have always dreamed of publishing a book. Now they have the book and want to know where to go from here. I've encountered authors with a business plan, and I've also run into authors who expected their book to "go big" once it was for sale online. The authors who know about the business and promoting side of publishing, and have plans to promote their book, do much better.

I think many authors are simply in the dark about what they need to do and how they can easily promote the book they've worked so hard on.

I was motivated to write this for three reasons:

1. I'm passionate about selling my own books and helping other authors succeed. I believe my knowledge, experience and ideas will help others.

2. I do a lot of research on book promoting. *A lot.* Most of the books and articles out there that I read do not cut it. It's like a hundred different writers read the same article and decided to paraphrase it on their own website. I read over and over again about sending books out for reviews and getting involved online, but most of the information doesn't go past this. The following pages will show you many more creative ways to promote your books. I believe you will enjoy applying many of these ideas.

3. I've picked up many books about book marketing. They're mostly written for people who are already on every online

networking site and have some knowledge of marketing. These books are a great resource for those people, but what about the authors who aren't internet savvy? What about the people who have dreamed of publishing a book and are doing so in retirement? And what about the vast number of people who know little about the changing publishing industry and what they need to do to promote their book? This book is for all of these people. I would love to share my knowledge with them.

In the end, it's word of mouth that spreads news about a book and generates sales. Imagine having a following of core readers who love your book and will tell others about it, post a review or mention it on their blog or other publication. Promotion is how you start that chain reaction.

Words of Wisdom

"A professional writer is an amateur who didn't quit."
—Richard Bach

"A famous author is a promoter who never quit."
—Kristin James

How This Book Can Help You

This book is written in quick, easy-to-read tips so you can find the ones that will help you. Alternatively, you can use this book as your book promotion plan, starting with tip one and moving through each step that will benefit you. All together, these tips show how you can constantly promote yourself as a writer.

Make sure to visit the blog at www.bookpromoting101.com for more articles and updates, or to share your book promoting successes.

If you read this book while writing yours…
You might find ideas about improving your hook or designing the book so it will sell better. You can begin promoting now, just as I began promoting this book as I wrote it.

Book Promoting 101 isn't about good writing, but you'll learn many aspects of marketing that you can incorporate into your books. That doesn't mean "writing to the market," but rather creating a book that is easier to promote.

If you read this while publishing yours …
It will help you prepare all your promotional ideas and material. This is an ideal time to work on your promotion plan, which may be simple and fun or more complex. That will up be to you. I'm here to empower you with knowledge about the publishing industry and book promotion.

If you have a publisher, a publicist or both, still be prepared to work with them to promote your book. Ask for advance copies so both you and your publisher can send them out.

If you read this after publishing your book …
You can still utilize many of these ideas to promote your book, and you will be even more prepared when you publish your next one. You can always run a new promotion, sale, event or giveaway and launch your promotion for all your current books.

Part 1: Promoting While Writing

What Makes a Book Tip?

Have you ever picked up a book, flipped through it or read it, and thought, "This book isn't that great. How did it get published in the first place?"

There are bestsellers that some readers say aren't well written. I recently read a best-selling book, and although I loved the story, I thought it was a women's fiction novel written in a choppy, male like writing voice. In fact, it was written by a male with many best-selling books under his belt, so name recognition probably had a lot to do with this case. The writing didn't work for me, yet the book tipped.

I believe books tip for two reasons: the writing and the promoting. If you have great writing and great promotion, your book can gain a readership.

Authors have a multitude of books, magazines, articles and websites about how to write well. I'll list some throughout this book and in the resource section. We can find writing partners, critique groups, writing groups and hire editors. With so many resources available, each of us can continuously improve as a writer even as we promote our work. Promoting is the other half of the formula.

While writing this book, I came across the following article and felt that it beautifully illustrates some of my ideas on marketing. It's a great starting point for anyone embarking on their writing and publishing journey.

Getting Your Book to the Tipping Point

by Stephen Blake Mettee

I was at the William Saroyan Writer's Conference recently when another presenter—Jack Canfield of *Chicken Soup for the Soul* fame—told me I needed to read Malcolm Gladwell's *The Tipping Point*. People are always telling me to read this book or that book, but I figured Jack probably knew a thing or two I didn't so I ordered the book from Amazon.com and read it on the plane coming and going to sales meetings in New York City. I think it was probably good use of what might have been wasted time.

In *The Tipping Point: How Little Things Can Make a Big Difference* Gladwell shows that three factors or "rules" as he calls them, combine to raise an idea, a trend, or a social behavior to a threshold that, when crossed, causes that specific idea, trend, or behavior to spread like wildfire.

Gladwell calls these three rules the Law of the Few, the Stickiness Factor, and the Power of Context. Gladwell's rules may be applied when trying to understand why one book and not another equally as good seems to reach the public's collective consciousness and becomes a bestseller.

Let's skip first to Gladwell's second rule, the Stickiness Factor. This rule suggests that something people hear or learn about a book must be extra memorable, it must be "sticky." This stickiness is often a minor part of the overall message in or about the book.

For instance, a recent biography of John F. Kennedy breaks the story that he had an affair with an intern while in office. While coverage of the affair is only a small part of the biography, it may well be that the parallel between JFK and a later president's affair with an intern will provide the stickiness required to make this book a bestseller.

Gladwell's third rule, The Power of Context, says the current social environment has to be ripe to embrace a specific principle or concept.

As I write this, I have on my desk a book proposal by an airline pilot on what one should do in the event one is a passenger on a hijacked airplane. Undoubtedly the social environment today is more receptive to this book's subject matter than it would have been prior to September 11, 2001.

Gladwell's first rule, The Law of the Few, states that a few people–the right few people in each instance–have the power to influence a great number of others. The few's currency is word-of-mouth, and, as we all know, word-of-mouth publicity is the best type of promotion a book can receive.

Gladwell breaks these few into three categories, "connectors," those who know and are able to spread the word to a large number of others; "mavens" who are looked to by others for advice; and "salesmen," who are capable of persuading others to take some action.

In publishing, the few often come in the guise of reviewers who write about the books, booksellers who hand sell books they like, and, perhaps not so surprisingly, the author of the book himself.

So, how can we who want our books to reach the tipping point use this information? By keeping these three factors in mind when we are writing and promoting our books.

As you write your book, see what kind of sticky material you can build into it. If it is a novel you are writing, maybe you can make the lead character so compelling that he or she becomes the stickiness factor. Sherlock Holmes, the pipe-smoking, clue-deducing detective provided stickiness for Arthur Conan Doyle's mysteries.

If you are still looking for a publisher or agent, mention this sticky material in your query letter or book proposal. If your book's due to be published, help your publisher's staff identify what detail or details about your book are likely to be "sticky" and suggest that they draw attention to these details in their catalog, back cover copy, news releases, and other promotional material.

Take advantage of The Power of Context by selecting a topic for your book that is currently high in the public's mind. The Big Seven–money, diet, health and fitness, beauty, relationships, sex, and power–are always good choices for nonfiction books, but, if you can find a popular but lesser-mined topic, all the better.

If your book's already written and published, spin or slant your promotional efforts to take advantage of the current social environment. For a nonfiction book on family values, talk about how important mutual family support is in these stressful times.

And finally, take your book to the all important "few." See to it that appropriate opinion makers such as reviewers, industry leaders, clergy members, university professors, and other authors who write in your field or genre know about your book. Do this by sending them complementary copies or, at the least, copies of reviews your book has garnered. Get as many print and Web reviews as you can. Get interviewed on radio and TV shows.

Augment all this by speaking at every bookstore and to every group that will have you. There is bound to be a connector, a maven, or a salesman in every audience who will become a word-of-mouth warrior on your book's behalf.

Reaching the tipping point isn't necessarily easy, but whose book deserves it more than yours?

Stephen Blake Mettee, author of The Fast-Track Course on How to Write a Nonfiction Book Proposal, *is the founder of Quill Driver Books and The Write Thought. He blogs at* TheWriteThought.com.

(Reprinted with permission.)

Creating a Buzz

If you're like me, you probably check your favorite authors' websites for updates. What are they working on? Do they have a new book coming out yet? Successful authors do not wait until the book is about to hit bookstores before they tell you about it. Any genre can really benefit from prepublication promotion.

People love to hear about what you're working on, so go ahead and tell fans a few interesting details.

Is your book a sequel? Or is your book the first in a possible series? Promote the series! Tell people the second one is in the works. Readers love series, and you can promote a book even before you write it in this case.

Does your book relate to any events past, recent or in the future? People love the History Channel and discovering new things about a famous event. You can promote just by telling people you're writing a book about the Civil War, or the history of your favorite sports team, or local history or even the history of your family. I live near Roseburg, Oregon, and many people write about the Roseburg Blast in 1959 when a parked truck loaded with two tons of dynamite and 4½ tons of nitrate exploded, destroying 23 blocks of downtown, leaving $12 billion in damage and killing 14 people. An author who lived through something like this has a story to tell.

If you're writing another form of nonfiction, promote how much the book will help readers. Can your book teach business owners how to raise profits or market better? As I wrote this book, I reached out to authors. I know the target group who will benefit most from *Book Promoting 101,* and I let them know about it early on.

If you put on your creative cap, you can come up with many ways to begin promoting a book before it's ready for press.

Have a Niche

I hear this from my husband all the time, and I know it's a sound, basic business idea. Think about it: Nike sells athletic shoes and Dell sells custom-built computers. When you look at a best-selling book, whether it's fiction or nonfiction, it has a specific focus. The topic is so brilliant and clear it's obvious. Well, it's obvious now that someone wrote the book. I see books all the time and think, *What an awesome idea! It's so obvious!*

I'll use the Twilight series as an example. It's about romance and vampires, which has grown into its own genre during the last few years. I just saw a section in the bookstore called *Teen Romantic Paranoia*.

A few years ago, you might have thought, "How can anyone write an original vampire book series? It's so overdone." The next thing you know, you're watching one of the Twilight movies and reading the book for the third time. It's obvious, but it's still a niche.

I wrote a novel about Native Americans for middle grade readers and up. You can't usually get away with adding, "and up" to your audience, but the story is written in a classic style that works for fourth graders, high schoolers and adults. The Native American fiction market is a niche. It's popular and has a steady following. Many universities and colleges have a Native American section in their online bookstore. Most self published books do not end up listed in a college bookstore, but my Native American novel did, simply because it's in a niche.

By writing for a targeted group, you'll actually hit more readers than if you try to write a book for every reader.

Diary of a Wimpy Kid is hugely popular with young boys.

Every book in The Clique series is a bestseller, created for young girls.

Even memoirs are a niche, if you employ popular themes with a new twist.

Join a Group

Most writers want to join a writing group for support, networking, feedback and meeting other people. It can be invigorating to talk about writing with other people who are passionate about it. Being in a group like this can improve your writing and provide new writing opportunities.

Some communities have a catchall group for writers. Some of these have smaller groups for different genres from fiction to short stories to nonfiction and others. In other communities, you might be able to find a group for your exact kind of writing, such as science fiction or romance.

So why is this tip in this book? How does a writing group help you promote your book?

- More people will know you write.
- More people will know about your book.
- More people will come by your book signings.
- More people will have a book signing with you.
- You will know about more events you can join.
- The group might have a website that will list your books, your website and your events.
- You might be able to get articles and stories in the newsletter or website with a bio mentioning your book and website.

It's highly beneficial to join any kind of group. Children's author Della Neavoll writes picture books about bugs. She was already a member of many local groups, including the Master Gardener's club. The members loved her book, especially because her volunteer work there taught her about bugs.

The Right Yes

As you're promoting your book and building excitement around you as a writer, you'll encounter periods where you feel frustrated and stalled. Other times you will be promoting with all these tips and feel as if it's not making a difference. Not everything you do will make a difference in sales soon afterward.

Each little thing you do adds up, however, and keeps your momentum moving forward. Sometimes you reach one reader who may very well be a key person to promote your book, and other times you might reach 20,000 people!

Keep in mind, while promoting online and making connections, one right yes can make all the difference. For example:
- A distributer says yes to distributing your book.
- A reading group decides to read your book for its book club.
- You're asked to speak to a large group or do an interview.
- A TV show covers your book.
- You get a good review in a big newspaper or trade journal.
- A well-known author writes a review on Amazon.
- A well-known reviewer reviews your book. (Some lay reviewers on Amazon carry a lot of weight, especially if people follow their blogs.)
- A publisher picks up your book!

How do you get to a big yes? By building upon the smaller successes. Think of your promotion plan in terms of steps, where you're building upward. When you go to a new step, like sending your book out for reviews, include previous reviews. This is just one of the tips you'll find in the following pages that will show you how to continually grow the buzz around your book.

Prepare to Promote

The best thing you can do to promote your book is to be ready. This holds true for authors with a big publisher or medium publisher and for self published authors.

The first step is to know what you're getting into.

The Ugly Truth
Even if you have a publisher, and your books are in stores, readers might not know to go look for it. If you're a new author, the publisher might not push your book. Your book might be placed on a display in stores, but it might also be placed on a shelf between other books where readers will quickly glance at the title.

If you have a book in bookstores, don't think you are done. Instead, realize you have a huge opportunity to sell your book if people find out about it.

This is even more true for self publishing. Don't think you can put any book on Amazon and then Oprah will call you. Millions of books are for sale online, and if you self publish one, no one will even know unless you tell them.

The Good News
The ugly truth is also the beautiful thing about publishing. *You can get a book out there, and you can make it successful with promoting.*

If you have a useful nonfiction book, a fascinating children's book or an engaging novel, you just need to get the word out. This is a vital step that many authors never take. It's sad when someone publishes a book but does nothing else with it.

There are three steps to sharing your ideas in book form: writing, publishing, promoting.

As an author, it's fine for you to toot your own horn. Actually, it's required if you want anyone to hear your music. Promoting means letting the world know about your book so readers can buy a copy and read it.

Considerations When Preparing to Promote:

- Do you have a promotion plan?
- Who do you know who can help promote the book? Do you know anyone working for a newspaper, in an industry that can use your book, or at a school, college or university?
- Do you know any bookstore owners?
- Do you know anyone working for a TV or radio station?
- Do you have family or friends who will be interested in your book's topic and want to help you spread the word?

A Rolling Snowball

Book promotion is like a rolling snowball. Every little thing you do to promote your book adds to the snowball. But when you drop the ball and forget about promoting your book, it all disappears. It melts.

It's true that you can generate big results if you can promote your book full time, but it's also true that you can do this by devoting an hour a day or doing one promotion task each day. When you do little and big things here and there to promote your book, it adds up to steady sales.

Little things include:

- Getting your book listed or mentioned in a new website, blog, article, or physical location
- Sending out a newsletter, email, or other communication
- Running an ad on Google or Facebook, or in a paper or other print publication
- Launching a new promotion, contest or giveaway
- Getting a reader or professional reviewer
- Speaking at or attending a writing conference
- Volunteering for a literary event, or any related event, where you can connect with readers, other authors and other people
- Speaking to a local writers' group, an online group or a readers' group
- Visiting a school (for children's books)
- Attending an event, making connections and displaying your book and name
- Publishing more books
- Winning a writing contest
- Winning a book award

Marketing experts know people are more likely to buy something they've seen in several places such as on TV, in a magazine and on the side of a bus. We see images all the time that make an impression. When readers have heard about your book or your name from different people, different ads, an article and other places, they might look up your website or book online, or they might even find the book in a bookstore. If they've heard about you and then see you at a bookstore, they're much more likely to buy your book.

Every little and big thing you do creates another impression. These add together online, putting you higher in search engines and building your presence. Name brands use these techniques to become household names. By promoting your work, you are branding yourself. If you're unsure of what I mean, think of Stephen King. Did you think of mushy romances? No, you thought of his horror books that have become movies.

Different authors have different brands:
- Nicholas Sparks writes Southern tragedies with a lyrical writing voice.
- Nora Roberts writes suspenseful romances.
- Agatha Christie wrote mysteries that are still popular.

If you think of yourself and your work as a product you are selling, it's easier to see why you would want to promote your writing as much as possible. If you love your writing, it can be fun to talk about it, write about it and connect with readers.

Being an author can be a blast, and many ways to market your book are fun. One of the easiest marketing tips I've ever heard is enthusiasm is contagious. Smiling is contagious. Smile and show your enthusiasm when you're talking to people, even on the phone. Did you know other people can tell when you smile over the phone?

If you feel discouraged while promoting, remember that promotion is like a snowball. You will probably see a rise in sales after events and promotions, and when you use the tips in this book. Afterward, sales will drop again. Don't give up! Later, you'll announce something new, and people will remember your earlier promoting and buy a book. Or maybe they'll hear about you for the first time and then see everything you've done. Think about promoting as a business but one you can have fun with.

Is Promoting Bad?

That question seems a bit silly since you're already reading this book. However, some people shy away from promoting because they fear it's wrong to push something they've achieved. *You shouldn't toot your own horn. You shouldn't let money taint your writing.*

Promoting, for the sake of this book, is getting the word out to the public so they will know about your book and read it. You wrote a book and now you want to communicate your message to readers. If you don't tell people about your book, they won't hear your message!

As authors, we get to reach out to strangers and connect with them in a special way.

Promotion is also about making money. You can choose one motive or both.

The truth is

"Without promotion something terrible happens... Nothing!"
—P. T. Barnum

If you're not familiar with P. T. Barnum, he was the great American circus entrepreneur who created "The Greatest Show on Earth" in 1871.

Barnum's wisdom applies throughout time and across industries. If you neglect to promote a new business, it fails. If you create a perfect wine and hide it away, no one will drink it. And if you write a book and decide promoting isn't for you, the book won't sell. Readers won't find it, enjoy it, or learn about your point of view or story.

Luckily, thankfully, you plan to promote your book, to shine the light on it and celebrate your work!

Change Your Mindset

I'd like to tell you a story about my husband and his great idea. While traveling in Europe, Lem noticed every park had a concrete tennis table, and he wondered why we didn't have them in parks in the United States. Over the next ten years he thought about starting his own business and even went to college for a business degree while working at a day job. After this, he worked in the parks and recreation industry for several years. An idea sparked and he decided to go for it. He would build and sell concrete table tennis tables. He would become an entrepreneur.

Soon he had designs on the computer and tables under construction. He designed a website, contacted park and rec managers across the country, made a Facebook page, advertised online and talked to everyone he knew. Then he officially launched his sales at a park and rec trade show in Seattle. There's been an overwhelming positive response to his idea.

Now imagine if he had build a concrete tennis table and put in at the edge of our yard with a FOR SALE sign on top. I'd bet you a hundred bucks he wouldn't have sold a table that way.

Why am I sharing this story? It's simple. Many authors do not realize they have a product that needs marketing.

As a published author, you are an entrepreneur.

Of course it makes sense to employ relentless marketing for any other new product or a business, but we turn around and think everyone we know will buy our book and tell all their friends about it.

Some writers seem to think that when a book is published, readers see it and buy it. Soon it's racing up the bestseller lists. Well, maybe we don't expect every book to go that big, but we often think books sell themselves.

Yes, it's true that a really good book will sell itself to some extent. If readers notice it in a bookstore, read it and tell others, it can spread. Some authors get to experience this. If you self publish, readers won't "just see" your book online. It's more important than ever to promote your book.

Read through that story again and pretend my husband was promoting a new book related to park management.

Imagine if you promote your book the way new business owners promote their businesses. They need to get the word out or their business fails. Well, guess what? If you don't promote your book, it won't sell. If you published it hoping to make a lot of money, you'll have to promote with the same fervor you wrote the book. Promoting can be fun; it can be a blast, but it needs to happen.

If your book is going to sell, *it needs to sell to complete strangers who see value in the book.* If you want your book to sell, you need to believe in your product and market it.

If you don't have a big budget, you can still invest time. I invest much more time than I do money in promoting my books. I'll show you how you can do this with the Internet and networking, both off line and online. You can do a lot of low-cost promoting too. A little money can make a big difference if you use it wisely.

If you have the money to buy ads, travel and promote in big ways, I'd still advise using your time to make connections. Get out there and enjoy being an author! Use paid promotion, but don't forget the personal side either. People love connecting with authors, learning about them and meeting them.

Research, read and learn about business marketing. You're taking a huge step in reading this book right now. I truly hope you'll find many ideas and fun ways to promote your book.

Start Early and Think BIG

Start Early

Start promoting your book before it hits bookshelves. If you're self publishing, start promoting before it goes online for sale. (You need to promote even more!)

Publishers promote the big names and books they're almost certain will make millions. They take a chance on newer authors but don't promote their books, knowing they will often lose money on most of these.

That means it's your job to get the ball rolling. Get advance copies from your publisher, gather names and addresses for reviewers, and send books out to newspapers big and small. Consider what kind of promotion your books needs.

As I was writing this book, I began promoting it. When it was two-thirds completed, I told authors about it and asked if they would review an advance copy. I reached out to an online friend, Paul Godines, who runs Adapt on a Dime. He offers coaching on book promotion and helps authors build a step-by-step plan for book success. He not only got excited about the book but also asked to interview me about my writing, publishing and book promoting. The interview is already live on his site and mine, with links on Facebook, LinkedIn and Myspace. I also emailed friends and family about it. I've mentioned the book in promotions for my other books too.

The cover is already done, and I'm designing promotional items with it. I have the cover shot in a publishing pamphlet ready to hand out at events. By the time this book is published, I plan to have people waiting to read it.

Many of these tips are very doable before your book is out. In fact, you will create a bigger buzz by promoting the book as early as possible.

Think Big

Your goal is to use a little promotion to reach as many readers as possible in your target market. If you can buy an ad for $1,000 that millions will see, that's a great deal. (An ad like that surely costs more, but you get the idea.)

I'll talk about Facebook ads soon because you can reach thousands of people with a very targeted ad. It's the biggest social networking site, and it's actually easy to use.

BIG promotion that you can do early includes sending your book out for reviews to newspaper, journals and anyone who will make a difference by writing about your book. TV and radio interviews are big. Advertise to libraries and bookstores as early as possible.

To think big, consider how to reach readers across the United States and even abroad, and remember to reach out locally as well. Thinking big may include:
- Entering a national novel contest (check out contests by Writer's Digest)
- Buying an ad in a national magazine that targets your audience
- Applying to speak at a large conference or event
- Getting involved in networking sites across the internet.

Thinking big also includes using each step and building to success.

"Putting out a newspaper without promotion is like winking at a girl in the dark—well-intentioned, but ineffective."
—William Randolph Hearst

"Ditto on Books."
—Kristen James

Know Thy Strengths

What is the best thing about your book?

If you know its strongest selling aspect, you're off to a great start.

To simplify the series Twilight, you could say it's about a human wanting to be a vampire, caught in the middle of a vampire and werewolf who both love her.

Here you have several strong selling points: vampires, wolves, a love triangle and a person with an overwhelming longing. It's easy to see why it's a best-selling series in paper and the big screen.

Your book might focus on a general theme and twist it in a new way. Highlight how you bring something new to the genre. Does your book offer something new to a popular genre? For example, my book *The River People* is Native American fiction featuring a young girl chief and a relativity unknown Native group.

For nonfiction, think about whom your book will help. Find a niche: how to raise tropical fish, how to train bird dogs, how to cook gluten free or how to overcome a specific problem.

A book might offer a new way of looking at the world, as many popular children's books do.

Notice these examples pertain to the book's marketing points, not your writing. Yes, it's very important to have and develop writing strengths such as dialogue, description and character development, but these are vague selling points. In reality, readers expect you to have these down, and they want to know what about your story will change them in some way.

List Ten Unique Aspects of Your Book

Here are questions to help you come up with selling points of your book.

- What genre is your book? (Being specific helps you sell it. A romantic science fiction fantasy epic nature story is hard to sell.)
- How does your book fit in with others in its genre?
- How is your book different?

Fiction

- What is the plot, in one sentence?
- Is it based on a real location, person or animal?

Example: *The Adventures of Star & Hiccups of Happy Valley* by Don Wood is based on a real horse and goat, which offers really fun promoting possibilities. Kids love learning about the animals behind the story.

- Did you add anything new to a common theme or genre?

Example: life after divorce, but the character has an unexpected windfall and life is completely complicated.

- Why will people want to read your book?
- What makes it different from other romances, mysteries or whatever genre it is?

Nonfiction

- Whom will this book help?
- What are your strongest selling points?

Elevator Speech

If you think an elevator speech is one you give in an elevator, you're partly on the right track.

Some think its name comes from a history of authors pitching their book to an editor or agent in the elevator, bathroom, sidewalk or other awkward place. This could be true. I know it happens.

A good elevator speech that will help you is a very short blurb about your book. It's the "teaser" in its simplest form, the trailer, the preview and something you will use all along as a way to promote your book.

For example:

"*Book Promoting 101* will help authors launch their book and sell more copies, even if they aren't on Facebook yet. The book teaches them how."

"*The River People* shows a young Native girl finding her place in the tribe, competing with her best friend and keeping peace in their valley when other braves invade."

I wouldn't stalk an editor and try to pitch my book in the bathroom at a writing conference, but you should have an elevator speech ready for your book. You can use it when:
- Anyone asks you what you're working on (while writing)
- Anyone asks what your book is about (they see you with it or just heard you're an author)
- An interviewer asks for a quick summary
- You approach a store owner or book buyer and need to capture her attention quickly

Having this ready enables you to get the book's idea out there and move on to why it will sell, who it will help, how well it's selling, why you wrote it and why you're qualified to write it.

If you look at best-selling books, fiction and nonfiction alike, you can probably generate an elevator speech. When you can do this for your book, you know you're headed in the right direction.

Tip: If you develop the elevator speech early in the writing process, it will keep you on track as you write.

You can expand your elevator speech into the query letter—editors and agents love a strong, clear hook. The query letter often turns into the back cover blurb.

You can also
- Expand it into the back cover blurb if you're self publishing.
- Post the short version on the top of promotional material or in online updates and comments.
- Expand it for your website and other promotional material.

The elevator speech is a quick and easy promotion tool with multiple uses.

Free and Easy

Many of the tips in this book involve spending a little money to make money. I strive to spend money only when I believe it will bring back a good return.

What is free?

It's free and easy to have an **email signature.** Go into your email, under settings, and set one up. Sometimes you can create a link so other people can click on it and go directly to your website or Amazon listing. If not, you can have your website address listed so people can copy and paste.

It's free and easy to **send out an email** about your new book. Prepare a professional press release and paste it in. Ask family and friends to forward it.

It's free and fairly easy to sign your books. Autographed books sell better from stores, so leave signed copies whenever you have an event. Romance author Katherine Sutcliffe climbed out of midlist to best-selling status by signing books by the thousands in the warehouse so they could be marked "Autographed Copies." This would take some time, but you can probably use this promotion method on a smaller scale.

It's free and easy to go onto Amazon.com to your book's page and list tags. If you have an Amazon account (you've bought anything through the site), you can scroll down the page and fill keywords into a box. Write in the most specific words related to your book. Look at other books to see their tags. For *The River People*, I have words such as Umpqua Valley, Native American Fiction, Pacific Northwest, Oregon and West Coast Indians.

It's free and actually easy to **use online networking** to tell people about your book. I'll cover how to join and use Facebook and even set up a free fan page for yourself or a free page for your book. There are many websites related to writing and reading too, such as www.goodreads.com.

It's free and fairly easy to **write a letter to the editor** of area newspapers. Make it quick and short. "Hello, I recently published a book on the history of our town." Of course, you can do this even if your book does not relate to any current events or location, but that does give you a reason for writing.

Example openings:

"I'd like to announce my new book is in stores."

"My second book is out this week. It's a suspense titled *Always a Widow, Never A Bride*. Every time she gets engaged, her fiancé is murdered or dies in an accident. What is going on?

"My newest children's book is available."

"I'd like to announce the publication of my first book."

Always include your website in these letters.

It's free to contact your local newspaper about doing a story on your book, a promotional event you're holding, a new award you've won or anything new and exciting related to your writing. To do this, you can call, write or email a news tip to the paper. It helps if you've networked with people working there.

It's free to write and submit articles on your book's topic. You can offer these to online blogs and websites in return for links to your website, if they don't pay. It can even be a source of income to submit articles to newspapers, magazines and online websites if you're an expert on your topic. Remember, being an expert often means you've done a little more research and have a few years' experience. Sometimes people are afraid of stepping out and offering advice, but you have useful information to share!

It's free to set up a blog, an Amazon author page and an author profile on different sites for readers. If you place your name and profile in different places online, you'll come up in more searches. You can build an online presence. Most people love connecting with others online, meeting new people from all over and keeping in contact.

It can be free to have a book signing. Ask the store managers if they can order copies of your book. Do this whenever you visit anywhere or take a trip.

It's free to give your time to speak at a school about writing or to make a helpful presentation about your book's topic to a group. This helps you network, sets you up as an expert and gets people excited about you, and it can be fun.

It's free to offer an interview. Reach out to bloggers, along with media such as TV, radio and newspapers.

It's free to network with other writers, readers and people who might want to work with you on a project or draw from your knowledge in your book's subject matter or in writing and publishing. One way to network is to help others.

In today's world, the creative person can find endless free ways to promote. The good news is anyone can be creative!

Now before you go overboard putting all your time into free promoting, you need a plan to direct your time, energy and money. The next tip is about writing your marketing plan.

Book Marketing Plan

This is your plan of action, checklist or business plan. It lays out all the steps you plan to take to promote your book. Your marketing plan will guide you, keep you on track and even work as a promotional tool.

Key Elements
- Short book description (sales pitch, back cover description)
- Target market—who will buy your book
- Your goal
- Marketing plan overview
- Specific steps
  - Distributors you will mail books to
  - Publications you plan to mail your book to for review
  - Radio and TV stations you will contact
  - Events, conferences, etc. you will attend

Let's go over a few of the items. (Some of this information might overlap with other tips, but that means it's really worth noting!)

Target Audience/Market
Your target market can't be readers, men, women or any broad group. If you consider the population of the United States, along with sales from best-selling books, you'll realize that even the most famous books do not reach an entire group of readers such as all men or all women. They reach a small target group of readers. Famous authors all have a following of readers who like their specific type of book and writing. Stephen King is one of the best known authors of our time, yet many readers do not like horror. The more specific you are about naming your target market, the more successful you will be in reaching them.

Think about it this way: if you can market to people who are very likely to buy your book, your investment of time and money brings a much bigger return.

Your Goal

Your goal might not be able to sell a million books. You might be writing a book that will appeal to a small group of people. Then your goal will be reaching that niche. You might be writing a book to raise awareness of a disease, condition or social issue, and you're not out to make a ton of money on it. In this case, you might be finding ways to donate books, give discounts and offer your book to groups for fundraising. Think about your goal for your book and let this temper and direct your efforts.

Overview and Steps

This is the nitty-gritty, action part of your plan. Here you will fill in information as you gather addresses and ideas. Look over the following marketing plan for ideas.

Tips
- Keep steps in chronological order.
- Write in dates, give yourself deadlines to keep things moving.
- Have your plan on the computer so you can fill in results and answers, in your own copy.
- Have a clean, professional copy that you will send out with your book when submitting to distributors and asking for reviews. This copy might not include all the details, but show your overall promoting plan. This shows others you're serious about promoting your book, and it works as a business plan that persuades them to invest in the book by ordering, stocking or distributing it.

Marketing Plan Checklist

Draw from this comprehensive list to create a marketing plan that works for you:

- Website
- Blog
- Press release
- Contact radio, TV
- List of newspapers to mail book to
- List of events in the next year that can benefit you
- List of contests to enter
- Entries for book awards
- Trade shows you can attend
- List of events that relate to your subject matter
- Writing groups
- Book clubs
- Article marketing (articles based on your book)
- Videos for your website
- Social networking sites
- Contests and giveaways you can run
- List of people you can help (Promote them and they'll remember you.)
- List of authors, media members or other people who will support you

The following pages offer a sample marketing plan for a real book so you can get a feel for this.

Sample Marketing Plan for *How To Enjoy Your Job.*
(Reprinted with permission.)

"How To Enjoy Your Job" (2008) by Joanna Penn

People hate their jobs. This book aims to change that.

"How to Enjoy Your Job" is an inspirational business/self-help book. It is aimed at the 50-70% of people who don't enjoy their jobs, and who are desperate to change their life but unsure how to.

The book outlines the results of modern working life including stress, depression and obesity. It tackles the main reasons people don't like their jobs: boredom, stress, lack of appreciation, trapped by money, other people and just being in the wrong job. The book is then packed with ways to improve your job, change your career or discover what you would really love to do with your life.

It is interspersed with anecdotes and inspirational quotes as well as practical tips and strategies. There is also a companion workbook available for download online at www.HowToEnjoyYourJob.com.

Overview

This plan contains the different strands of marketing that would go into the campaign for "How to Enjoy Your Job."

Target Market: Office workers aged 26-50 who commute to work. Women as they primarily buy self-help books.

Timing: The various angles would be pursued concurrently so that maximum impact is gained by multiple exposures in multiple media. To be running at least 1 month after hard launch.

Cost: Free and low-cost strategies would be pursued primarily with paid advertising/PR/marketing kept to the most effective usage.

PR/ Publicity

Press Kit
- Set up press kit on the website with audio and video links
- Include press clipping of publications and articles already published
- Have press pack that catches attention, e.g. cafeteria with mug "Love your job like you love your coffee"

Local Papers, Radio and TV Stations
- Play the local angle of the new author. Write the article for them.
- Brisbane XTRA TV show for local news
- Send copy to the lpswich major, Paul Pisasale, as he is active in the media

National Papers, Radio and TV
- Target MX with free giveaways as they as filled with unhappy commuters who hate their jobs
- Press releases to national press targeting cities and career pages

Book Reviewers
- Send copies to book reviewers in various publications
- Send review copies to book clubs with large distribution

Testimonials and Endorsements
- Get cover quotes from famous people quoted in the book
- Put testimonials on other people's websites with my website address on them as link backs

Press Releases
- Send multiple press releases related to stories in the media through Australian Ass. Press and direct to targeted journalists
- Send press releases based on timings: e.g. common New Year's resolutions is to change jobs

Print Articles
- Submit articles for print media on related subjects
- Article in Working Woman—Spring 2008 on career change

Speaking
- Run workshops for companies and include the cost of the book in the price of the seminar
- Volunteer for local associations and organizations that need speakers
- Practice "elevator" speech for quick pitch
- Build slides of key points of book so I can produce these as part of speaking

Networking
- Active member of Women's Network Australia who have the book on their bookstore online
- Sell at networking events
- Member of Australian Businesswomen's Network
- Build brand and reputation as an author and sell book at events as well as talking about it

Book Launch and Local Bookstores
- Launch at independent bookstore. Make sure media are aware. Press release before and after.
- Approach local and independent bookstores to see if they will buy books
- Donate books to local library and offer to speak
- Sell at fairs and markets in person

Promotional Material
- Have book cover and free offer on business cards and hand them out whenever possible
- Wear T-shirt with book image and name on as well as website
- Stick stickers or stamp with website name on all posts

Internet Marketing

Main website: www.howtoenjoyyourjob.com
- Optimize main site to capture email addresses and encourage direct sales with free workbook
- Sale of book in multiple media—ebook, audio and print book
- Testimonials for credibility
- Free articles with resources box available

Articles
- Post regularly on top article websites EaineArticles.com and Articlesbase.com that syndicate across the web

Amazon.com
- Do Amazon.com book reviews on similar topics with links to my book
- Add Amazon blog and all testimonials to site, plus new cover
- Add video to my Amazon page
- Promote sales through my affiliate AStore

Blog and Social Networking
- Drive traffic to my website and encourage sales through my blog at www.JoannaPenn.com
- Facebook profile has link to website and promotes book
- LinkedIn profile has info on the book as well as the day job
- Set up a lens on squidoo.com
- Channel on YouTube for book related videos
- Post free information and useful documents on Docstoc.com for search engines
- Profile on AuthorsDen.com
- Submitted on Authonomy.com

Word-of-Mouth and Viral Marketing
- Add a Tell a Friend button to website
- Post videos on YouTube with excerpts from the book, advice
- Create a screensaver for YouTube with inspirational quotes and the website address
- Add signature file with book free offer and website to all emails

Targeted Internet Advertising
- Run ad campaign on common words for people changing jobs, looking for job advice on Adwords. Can be country and city specific advertising.
- Use targeted Facebook advertising which can be directed to age group, gender, interests as well as location

Build Database for Email Marketing and Auto-Responders with Free Giveaway
- Free workbook is available for download at www.howtoenjoyyourjob.com
- Email addresses are captured and 10 auto-responders are sent to the people over the period of 1 month, encouraging them to use the workbook and buy the book
- Periodic emails blasts on interesting topics and blog posts

Utilize Affiliates
- Set up affiliate program where people can earn commission on referrals to the website for sales

Measure and Optimize Marketing Activities
- Use Google Analytics to track traffic and conversation rates and measure success
- Measure Google Adwords campaign and tweak adwords as necessary
- Measure traffic to blog and use keyword finder to blog with searchable terms

Joint Ventures

Work With Similar Authors to Joint Promote
- Target similar authors for co-promotion
- For example, I have been a featured author on an American business communication program which gained me traffic and sales
- I have also been a guest speaker on a new book "Job Interview Strategies" and I have a giveaway in their program that directs traffic to my website

Be Part of Compilation Books Which Promote My Own Book in the Resources Box
- I have a chapter in "Living an Abundant Life" (published Oct. 2008) which also includes Jack Canfield, Mark Victor Hansen, Neale Donald Walsch, Wayne Dyer and Brian Tracy amongst others. My chapter includes my website www.howtoenjoyyourjob.com.
- I also have excerpts in another compilation book promoting female entrepreneurs called "Sprout the Life you Love"

Blog Guests
Invite other authors and business people to be guest blogs or interviews on my blog. The reciprocate and promote me.

Corporate Sponsorship and/or Mass sales
- Approach companies to buy for their employees or clients as corporate gifts, e.g. recruitment companies, seek.com and similar
- Direct marketing to libraries for self-help/careers section
- Universities and careers offices for bulk buy
- Australian Institute of Management has a library and a book sales service. Approach them with on-sell opportunity.
- Life Coach Institute for sales to life coaches for their clients
- Employee Assistance Programs as they have unhappy employees as clients

Charitable Tie-In

- Charity is Outward Bound Trust (10% of Profits)
- Press release on the impact of Outward Bound tying into book
- Charitable event with proceeds to Outward Bound

Contact Details

Joanna Penn – Business Consultant, Author and Speaker

(e) joanna@TheCreativePenn.com

(w) www.HowToEnjoyYourJob.com
(Blog) http://www.TheCreativePenn.com

Your Book Cover

Are you designing your own cover, working with a company to design your cover or at least having a say in your cover design? Read this section first!

If you're self publishing, this section is critical to your book's success.

Your book cover is like an ad and business card rolled into one; a front-cover design can make or break your sales. There are many avenues you can take in getting your cover. In most cases, this should not include photoshopping your own photos and overlaying text. The biggest mistake I see with self published covers is I can tell they have one picture for the background and a smaller one in front with blurred edges. This would be a good starting point if you took this to a professional illustrator as an idea template. They could then draw a cover to match your concept.

I've seen poets self publish their poetry and make beautiful books, but for some reason it doesn't work as well for fiction. Find a local company or go online and hire a professional to design your cover. If you go through a self publishing company, find one that has design tools or offers design services. Some even include this with your book package. A cover designer has a feel for what works and sells books.

These days, online sales are overtaking bookstore sales. This means your cover should show up well as a small picture on the computer screen. Is the title readable? Does it grab your attention? Keep this in mind when designing your cover.

Childrens' authors can have their illustrator paint the cover or they can use an interior painting, and fiction writers can hire an illustrator for the job.

For bookstore and in-person sales, your *back* cover is a powerful marketing tool. Here are a few secrets:

- Go to your bookshelf and look at several back covers. You will notice novels published in the last ten years do not have the title on the back cover. The reader already read the title on the front and now wants a reason to buy the book. Putting the title here wastes space. Instead, put a review or the biggest hook of the book on the top of the page.

- This leads into the second secret. Do not tell readers that the book "will change your life" or "keep you hooked till the last page." Put in over-the-top claims only if they come from a celebrity or authority and you can cite them with the review.

- Stick with the biggest selling point: how a nonfiction book helps readers or, for fiction, the big question in the book such as "Can Cora trust the enemy's son long enough to find her father?"

- It looks better to have fewer words and some space as opposed to cramming text from the top to bottom of the back cover. Have a grabbing headline at the top, an intriguing description and a short bio. A short bio takes less space and forces you to include information relevant to why you're qualified to write the book. You can have a larger photo and longer bio inside the book. Use the back cover to highlight items that will persuade readers to buy the book.

- Lastly, design the cover together. A book really has a wrap around cover that includes the front, the spine and the back. Sometimes elements carry over. If so, they should match up. Look at the wrap around cover and finished product to determine if you book presents a professional look.

Attributes of Success

I've always enjoyed reading the bios of highly successful authors. When I started out, I searched for stories of how each author first sold a book, met their agent or got their start. People like to share the story of when they realized they had made it. One of my favorite how-to books on writing and publishing is called *How To Write and Sell Your First Book,* by Oscar Collier with Frances Spatz Leighton. This book showed me how to get started back when I was a teenager dreaming of being a published author. Chapter 10 is called "They Weren't Always Superstars: How Six Famous Novelists Got Started." Whereas the book taught me how to write a query letter and properly submit it, these stories educated and inspired me.

These days I look for promotion and marketing success stories. With the changing industry, success these days comes by getting a great book out there and letting everyone know about it.

We can learn a great deal by watching how others succeed. In the following article, the author lists attributes he has witnessed in successful authors he knows. I found myself identifying with some of these things and I hope you do as well.

The 7 Attributes of Highly Successful Authors

by Bob Baker

(This column first appeared in the St. Louis Publisher's Association newsletter.)

Are you a curious person? I am. Especially when it comes to people who have taken action to achieve worthy and creative goals. Whenever I meet a successful author, musician, artist, actor or whatever … I try to find a way to pick his or her brain and discover what the person did to breathe life into their aspirations. I also pay attention to the qualities and traits that the most successful people seem to have in common.

Through the St. Louis Publisher's Association and other networking opportunities, I've been blessed to get to know several successful authors. I believe that taking what I've learned from them, and combining their strategies with my own views and methods, has greatly helped me to become a full-time, self published author.

With that in mind, here is a list of what I consider to be the seven attributes demonstrated by the most successful authors:

1. **They're on a mission (or at least feel they have something to say)**. Many prominent authors write because they have to. What drives them goes far beyond money and recognition. They write and share their words because they have a story that needs to be told, a point of view that needs to be communicated, a message they feel the world needs to hear. To be successful, you must become an evangelist for your topic.

2. **Their vision is stronger than the rules and obstacles they encounter**. I don't have to tell you that there are a ton of hurdles that aspiring authors run into. Many of them are tangible (such as editing, prepress and distribution matters) while others are mental barriers (like the fear of rejection, financial struggle and anticipated prohibitive costs to enter the field). What sets apart successful authors is their almost naive,

child-like ability to not buy into common myths and let their greater vision guide them around any obstructions they encounter.

3. **They understand the "self" of self-promotion**. No matter what level of success you attain, you will always be intimately involved in the promotion of your books. Struggling writers wish they could hand off the marketing work to someone else so they can concentrate only on the writing. Sure, you can hire a publicist or assistant to help with some things, but no one will ever promote you as passionately as you can. To succeed, get on friendlier terms with promotion.

4. **They make the best use of available tools**. There are all sorts of ways to create, market and sell books these days. There are traditional methods such as sheet-fed printers, distributors, bookstores, trade magazine reviews, bulk sales to associations, etc. And there are relatively newer options at your disposal: print on demand, web sites, e-zines, Amazon's Advantage program, blogs, podcasts and more. You don't have to use every option (and probably shouldn't for sanity's sake). But you should at least be aware of what's available and choose the best new and old tools for your book topic and personality.

5. **They put a focus on readers and fans**. What's the number one factor that determines an author's material success? Is isn't the size of his publisher or the reputation of his agent. It isn't the amount of her advance or the raving reviews she gets in the press. The only thing that matters is the number of people who purchase and read the book and then rave about it to their friends. The most successful authors understand this and always put a priority on attracting and retaining readers … and turning readers into fans.

6. **They think of themselves as a personal brand with a clear identity**. People may at first be attracted to the title and subject matter of your book, especially when you're a new author. But if they really enjoy what you've written, they will start to associate your name with the benefit you deliver through your books. Then, instead of looking for another book on your topic, your fans will seek out other books by you. Most of the top authors are known for a specific subject or genre, and once

established, they crank out a series of similar books. You should consider doing the same.

7. **They understand that being a solo author doesn't mean working alone**. The author's life can be a solitary one—particularly when immersed in writing a new book. But successful authors realize that writing alone doesn't mean they have to be lonely or feel like it's them against the cold, cruel world. Even solo self published authors can (and should) share ideas with other writers and assemble a team that might include editors, graphic artists, web designers, print brokers and more.

There's my list of the seven success attributes. How does it compare with your list? If I missed anything, feel free to shoot me an email with your thoughts. I may include your comments in a future article or blog post.

Bob Baker is the author of *Unleash the Artist Within, Guerrilla Music Marketing Handbook* and *Branding Yourself Online*. Get a FREE subscription to Bob's newsletter, *Quick Tips for Creative People*, featuring inspiration and low-cost self promotion ideas for artists, writers, performers and others. Visit PromoteYourCreativity.com for details.

Part 2: Before You Publish

We covered many ways to promote while you are writing your book, and guess what? There's even more ways to promote as you prepare the book for press.

Traditional authors have a year or two to promote while their book is being edited and proofed. This time is well utilized by blogging, speaking, promoting other books and finding creative ways to create a buzz for your upcoming book. (Don't forget writing!)

Self published authors can often get their book print ready faster because they're working on one book (instead of a publisher working on several). If you're self publishing, don't neglect editing, proofreading and professional cover design. You can find these services through freelance websites, or you can turn to professionals you know such as teachers, professors or journalists. Quality is important, and having a well-written, professionally presented book will make promoting all that much easier and more successful.

**However your book will be launched into the world, promote it
early!**

Promote the Package

People love celebrities. We watch their movies, read their websites and twitter updates, and read about them in news updates and sometimes even the tabloids.

Do you think of yourself as an entertainer? As a celebrity? If you said no, why not?

You're creating a product that is meant to entertain people, among other things. Even if you write nonfiction, you want to engage your readers to the point that they'll enjoy reading your book cover to cover. You can be a celebrity at many different levels.

So what is the package? And how do you promote it? You and your books are the package. Even if you didn't realize it until now, you are actually promoting you, your writing, you as a writer, and your books all at once. It's time to put on your celebrity hat and promote the package!

Think of your favorite authors. Can you picture them? Think of some of their best work? I know the stories of my favorite authors—when they got THE CALL and sold their first book, what motivated them to write and what they're doing now. I like to learn about them and their life. Of course, I don't know private details, but I know the public author, the celebrity.

Be ready to share with readers why you started writing, why you wrote this particular book, about the writing life, your dreams and what helps you as a writer. Finishing and publishing a book are two milestones to celebrate, and discussing them with readers is another reward as an author. What did the reader get out of the book? What did they think of the characters? Sometimes readers have discussed my books with me and showed me something I didn't see!

Promoting the package works in your favor in many ways.

- It's fun!

- Not only is your book out there winning fans, but you can win readers over with your charisma, your articles on writing, your presentation and your overall presence.

- If your short story places in a contest or gets published, you can use this to promote all of your writing. (Any good news can promote you and all of your writing.)

- Every good thing adds to your writing credentials. The real package is you as a writer, so, by promoting yourself, you are promoting your books and pushing sales.

- Your name becomes a brand for your quality writing.

- Celebrity power is always a good thing. Use it! Act like you are an entertainer and readers are waiting for your next book. Always be ready to talk about your writing and what you're working on. The public wants to know!

Build on Success

In life, it might annoy people if you keep a list of every compliment you ever get and post them on your website, office wall, Facebook, and vehicle. It's a little different when you're promoting a book. Think about it: don't you check the reviews in a book? I look for ones that say something different than, "5 star!" or "Highly Recommended!" I want to know why the book is so great. When I visit an author's website or a website for a book, I check out reviews and all the press. It really shows something to have links to five news articles about the book and reviews. With this in mind, collect and share reviews for your book, articles about it or other press that will help your cause.

Now every time you have a positive response, a review, a mention in the paper or anything else related to your book, save it. Put links on your website. Use everything you can and build upon it. All of these items can go into future press releases, ads, posters, and emails. You don't have to carpet bomb the internet with your promotion every day, but you can mention these when you send out an update about a new event or book.

When you have success with a tip from this book, use it as a step to another positive level. If you collect five reviews for your media kit, you can then send your book to a larger newspaper or magazine. Your previous success shows the book's merit so it will get more attention.

Every success adds to the inertia of your snowball. This is how you add to your ever growing platform so your book will snowball into wild success.

Celebrity Endorsements

Do not skip this tip, thinking you can't reach a celebrity or that you don't know anyone. (This information mostly pertains to nonfiction authors, but there is information for fiction writers afterward.)

Your celebrity does not need to be Oprah or Stephen King. There are countless people with celebrity power who are much more accessible.

If you know anyone who is an expert in your book's subject area, by all means, ask if that person will review an early copy of your book, write a review or endorse it. If you have ties to anyone in the media or someone whose endorsement would bring value to the book, call that person.

I have read several accounts of authors who wrote about someone they knew yet did not think to have the person endorse the book. Perhaps you mention someone in your book and could ask that person to review and endorse it. When you know the person, sometimes all you need to send is the book, after discussing it with him or her.

If you don't have any ties to someone you want to endorse your book, you can go about getting endorsements another way. Celebrities are asked to endorse things all the time, so their publicists are used to this. First you need to find contact information through their company, agent, website or a business directory. Be polite and don't try to contact them at home!

It might be the case that this person provides an email address online and is happy to talk to people. I've been surprised at how well people respond to a professional and courteous email. I will explain how I found his information and how I know him (I follow his blog or read his articles) and then I present my idea.

If the person agrees, send your media kit with a cover letter, a press release, book description, any reviews you already have, the book's synopsis and the book itself. You can even include a sheet of sample endorsements—the reviews you would like that person to write. She can circle one and mail it back to you. Yes, this actually is the way it works sometimes.

The Internet has made the world such a small place that you can usually get in contact with someone through a website or blog, if she's not a huge movie star or bestselling author. Maybe there is a business person or public figure who would be interested in your book. You'll greatly increase your odds of success if you approach someone who would be interested in your subject matter.

Are you a fiction author? If you've been networking with other authors—through your writing group, conferences, events, online or some other way—then you can ask celebrity authors about reading and endorsing your book or writing a review or just giving you feedback.

Celebrity endorsements are an underused method of promoting books, but they are not impossible to get. Imagine the effect an endorsement would have on your sales!

Your Website

Yes, some of you are scared of the work or cost involved in setting up a website. For your first book, you can get away with a free website, and you can get help in setting it up from friends, family or even your kids if they're old enough. I've met several older authors who had a grown child help them with new technology.

The websites www.blogspot.com and www.wordpress.com both allow anyone to set up a blog for free. You can easily post new stories, articles and blogs for others to read. As you learn more, you can add pictures and extras on the site of your blog.

Many sites help you set up an account and build a website from templates. For example, www.mysite.com allows you to easily build a site for free if you purchase the domain name. As of late 2010, it runs $20 a year for this. If you have one or two books out, this is a great option.

With www.yahoo.com, you can get started for $13 to $15 a month with a site that will give you a custom email address. Yahoo offers several design tools (programs), so you can choose how involved you want to be. It also offers website-design services.

Many authors talk to others people who already have a website. This can guide you in choosing your provider and setting up your site.

I still maintain my own websites. I could hire a company to design them, but I'm creative and like to be in control. I enjoy updating my sites all the time and changing them when I feel like it.

You may enjoy the creative aspect of designing your own website if you have a talent for design, or you might reach a point where it's worth it to pay someone.

Choosing a Web Address

On the surface, this seems like a no-brainer. You probably noticed my website address is my name. Most best-selling or well-known authors use their name as their website address too.

You have several options, and each has its place. First, let's discuss using your book's title as your web address.

www.yourbook'stitle.com
If your book is called *Finding Mr. Right*, you might want your website to be www.findingmrright.com. People hear about the book and Google it, finding your website right away. It's how we find other products, right? We search for the product's name.

Many nonfiction books use the book title for a website address. The information offered in the book is often more important to readers than the author's name is.

Another time it's wise to use the book's title is when it's your first book and it's doing well. To tell the truth, *any* time any of your books is doing well and bringing in money, it should have its own website.

That's a subtle way of saying; you can have an author website plus another website for a book. That makes it easier for readers to find you or the book if they search with the book's title.

A Series
If you have a series of books on a given topic, you might elect to use the series' name for the website. If you're written ten books about organic gardening, try www.organicgardening.com. When someone looks for one of the books, she will learn about all ten.

Your Name as a Brand
This brings us back to using your name as a website address. If you want to be a career author, this is the way to go. You can still set up websites for different books to promote them further. A website with your name as the address provides a central online location for your bio, updates, news of upcoming events, stories and information on all

your books. If they want to look up a certain romance author or science fiction author, readers probably want to find all this information in one place.

Another way to use multiple locations online is having a website and a Facebook page. Each of your books can have its own Facebook page, depending on how much time you have to put into creating Facebook pages. (Yes, there is a tip on this later on.)

Your online presence can include a website, a blog, Facebook pages, LinkedIn account, and accounts on other sites. It depends on how much time you have and where you want to invest it.

Content
Your website should promote you and your book or books but don't stop there. You can share short stories, fun facts, announce events, share pictures from events and reader feedback. The more fun you have with your website, the more interested readers will be. Take some time to browse author websites online. What attracts or impresses you? What bores you? Notice the websites that offer more than a blurb about the book.

Soon I'll share a tip called "Content is King," which tells about what attracts readers to author websites.

Website Designing

If you have ever designed a card or flier on a computer, you're ready to build your own website. Many people love the creative aspect of this, and it isn't too hard if you use computers. If you don't, there is probably someone in your life who does and would help you.

Another way to find help with anything, including designing your own website, is to Google it or search on eHow. If you go to www.ehow.com and enter specific searches, you can get a great article or video showing you exactly how to do it.

For example, if you enter, "How to design a website on Yahoo," it will provide articles that are very specific to Yahoo. I recently wanted to make a screen shot of a webpage. I searched on eHow and learned how to save an exact copy of the webpage I was looking at with two buttons.

When designing your site, many programs will have you enter your site's purpose and then choose a background. If you enter "writing/editing," you'll find templates with books, pens and writing-related images.

Most sites will have several pages you can customize or they will show you how to fill in information in the right places.

Still unsure of designing it yourself?

There are countless options for hiring a company or freelancer to design your website for you. Most best-selling authors hire a company to design, host and update their website while the author writes, blogs, goes on book tours and drinks martinis with her agent. (Well, I can't back up the martini part, although Kristin Hannah posted pictures of a party at her agency.)

Many people will argue that professionally designed websites look much more professional, and I agree this is true in many cases.

Biz Cards, Bookmarks and More

There's a common idea that writers should have business cards and bookmarks made up right away to hand out. These do come in handy when someone asks you about your writing, but don't spend too much on them. I consider them the basic promotional items, but not the fun promotional items. I'm all about fun things. Bookmarks can be fun if you think people will use them and give them out for you.

I advise authors to have a business card but also use their money on fun and useful promotional items that people will actually want. If you carry your books with you, you might not need a card!

Paying for promotional materials?
These can be fun to design, fun to have and share, and they can gain you exposure. The trick is to get a big return; meaning you can get new customers and sell books by using them. So, beware that you don't spend a fortune on promotional items to sell a few books. Spend money on things you can reuse or ads that will get a lot of exposure.

I'm mentioning Vistaprint because it's helped me so much. I use www.vistaprint.com to create many promotional products at a very low price. This site offers free business cards if you pay shipping, or you can pay a little extra to upload your own picture or designs. The site also sells custom coffee cups, pens, biz cards, t-shirts, hats, key chains, websites, magnets for the fridge, big magnets for your car, calendars and bags. (See the next tip.)

If your book is coming out in stores and you're making money, you might want to consider spending some on giveaways such as these. If you're not working with an advance, you can purchase promotional items for your own use, where people will see them.

I design two-sided biz cards there, and I just received a custom pen with my name, website address and email address. I paid a buck for shipping. I plan to use it at signings just because I thought it looked nice. If you expect to make many book sales at an event, you could possibly give some away.

How to Use Promotional Items

So how do you use all these ideas without spending your whole paycheck on them?

Don't give every person at a book event a free coffee mug. Give one away, filled with candy. Or use promotional items as a raffle prize or for people who buy three or more books.

Some of these items work best if you buy and use them so people will see them. Think of a giant magnet on your car or your book cover on a mug, T-shirt or bag.

Be creative, think outside the book and find a unique method. How can you promote your book while helping people? Is there something you can put your book cover on that people will use, see and give away? Is there a way to get your book cover out there where many people will see it? Check out my next tip: putting your book cover on a tote bag.

Bag It!

Women love bags. If you're like me, you might have ten purses and bags in your closet right now.

Now picture a canvas tote book bag with your book cover proudly displayed, along with its title in big, bold letters.

A bag is like a mini billboard!

Once you have your bag, you can carry copies of your book with you everywhere, while advertising it.

If you have several books available, you can create a picture to promote them, with your website address. If you're creative on the computer, design a small poster and use it on your bag as well. See the next tip, "Sales Sheets," to see one that I created. I use mine on fliers and have submitted it for an author's booklet at a book fair I attended.

How to Get Them

You can print these up at a local print shop, www.vistaprint.com, Walmart and many other camera and department stores. You can even order iron-on pictures of your cover or a full-page iron-on that displays your cover along with the title and your name underneath.

You can use these bags to promote in other ways too.

- Fill a custom bag with your book and other new books and raffle it at a book signing, group signing or literary event.

- Give away a bag to the first two customers or to people who buy five or more books. (I would iron on the picture to an inexpensive bag for this. Be careful that you aren't spending way more money than you can make on your books.)

- Carry your books in this bag so you have them ready when people ask you about it.

Media Kit

I've discussed sending your book out to book reviewers, and this is what you send with it. A media kit contains:

- A press release
- Your sales sheet with book description and bio
- Your reviews
- Praise for your book
- Promotion plan (marketing plan)

Need help with these items? I explain them in other tips.

You can begin building the book's media kit before it hits bookshelves. Before you publish, send out advance copies of your book. Send these to newspapers near and far and to people in your network who have some authority to say this is a good book. Collect all of these for your media kit.

You can still add to your media kit after you begin using it. In fact, you should continue to build it with new press, new reviews, awards and updates.

A media kit greatly increases your chances of getting a review. You can send it to newspapers to encourage them to write a story about you. It provides content that you can reuse on your website and in promotions. It's a resource to you and anyone in the business who looks at your book. Send it to stores when you ask them to stock your book. Use it when you interview.

Create Sales Sheets

Sale whats? Sales sheets can stand alone as a flier you pass out, or they can appear as an ad in the paper or in a booklet at a book fair.

A sales sheet should contain your book cover or covers if you're promoting more than one, your name, website address, book description(s) and if you have room:

- Your bio
- An explanation of why you wrote the book
- Reviews or an excerpt from a review
- A statement on what makes this book different from others

This is like a press release, but a sales sheet is colorful and usually printed on shiny paper.

You can print a sales sheet on shirts, bags and fliers and inside books, and you can enlarge it and print it as a poster. A print shop can do this for you.

A sales sheet is like the cover letter to your media kit. It's flashy and fun.

If you design your own sales sheet, keep it handy on your computer. The sales sheet is a great starting point for designing a poster to promote a book signing.

Kristen James

www.writerkristenjames.com

Kristen James has three published novels and another under consideration. She writes young adult, romance, women's fiction and short stories. She also owns and operates Bravado Publishing. She and her husband live on the N. Umpqua River and have six children between them. Her hobbies include cycling, running, reading, camping, berry picking, fishing, hunting and going on fun adventures with her kids.

kristen@writerkristenjames.com

The Herald and News of Klamath Falls called *The River People* "A nicely told tale that discusses American Indians from a different perspective. It combines history with romance, with a hint of early women's liberation, and a larger dose of Indian culture."

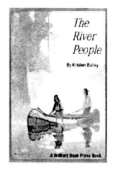

"*A Cowboy for Christmas* is a great romance for the holidays or anytime you like. Real flaws are found in Brent and Missy which result in the great journey this couple takes on. Humor and strength are also found in the pages of this book. A bit fun and flirty read that will not disappoint."

Call Your Local Newspaper

I'll talk about getting reviews later, which is different than getting a feature story in your local paper. For now, how do you get your newspaper to write a story on your book?

When to contact papers, TV, radio
- When you sell a book to a publisher
- Right before the book will hit stores
- Right when your book will hit Amazon and/or bookstores

Have a press release ready. (See the following tip.)

Give the paper a free book, along with your press kit.

Have a HOOK. What is a hook? It's a magical type of manna that floats down from publishing heaven. It's the strongest selling point of your book, and often you should have several. The main conflict of the book is a hook. The reason you wrote the book is a hook, especially if it's something emotional such as a life-changing event. This is true even for fiction. Your hook gives the papers and radio and TV station a reason to cover you.

Imagine: "This is Evan Kline, who wrote *Missing Emily* about the disappearance of his five-year-old daughter. It chronicles his trials and emotional journey as he spends three years looking and finally finds her."

This hook is a combination of the author's motivation and a great story.

Hooks do not have to be so dramatic to deserve attention. Many of the authors in my home region have books with local hooks, such as one related to the wine industry here, some about Bigfoot (a Northwest favorite) and others about native birds.

Consider contacting all the local papers where you live and papers where you have lived in the past, especially your childhood home.

Write a Press Release

A press release is an important part of your book promotion. You'll use press releases throughout your writing career to announce a new book, event or something big enough to interest the media.

Now you'll be preparing one to announce the publication of your book.

What is it?
The press release is one page and tells papers and TV and radio stations the hook of your book, something about you and maybe why you wrote it.

What does it do?
When you send out a press release, hopefully people will contact you to do a story about your book. The paper may do a write up. The TV station may do a story if you have something very interesting about you and your book. It entices readers into finding out more, which means you use it a bit like a sales sheet.

How to Use It
You can send out a press release to announce a book launch, book signing or other event. Include press releases in your media kit.

A press release can double as other promotional material. Rewrite, reuse or simply copy the information into an email to announce your book, and use it on your website and sales sheets.

Press Release Format (Some elements can vary)

FOR IMMEDIATE RELEASE -- Date

(Title of Release) Local Author Writes Book About Duck Hunting

Quick teaser to book: very short, grabbing description

Second paragraph: longer description

Third paragraph: your interesting bio, why you wrote the book, what relates you to book topic or makes you an expert

Contact:
Your name
Your email address
Your mailing address
Your phone numbers

(These symbols end the press release.)

The following page is the press release for this book. (It prints on one legal size sheet, but for this book it runs into two pages.)

FOR IMMEDIATE RELEASE – March 1, 2011

New Book from Author and Publisher Shares How to Tip Book Sales

Book Promoting 101: How to Tell The World About Your Book (Even if you're not on Facebook yet)
By Kristen James, owner of Bravado Publishing

Book Promoting 101 shares a wealth of tips and information about promoting a new a book in person, online, through networking and advertising. The 140 page book includes information about today's publishing industry, the new POD method of publishing and printing books and the Kindle market. Priced at $9.99, this small investment will equip authors to gain reviews, exposure, support and multiply their book sales.

Book Promoting 101 offers information on publishing and guides authors through promoting:

Part 1: Promoting While Writing
Part 2: Promoting Before You Publish
Part 3: Your Book Launch
Part 4: The New Publishing World
Part 5: Success Stories and Resources

This book shares:
- How to build a marketing plan
- How to sell books online and in person
- How to set up a website and blog
- How to use Facebook, online social networking and marketing
- How to attract readers to your website
- How to use both professional reviews and reader reviews
- Tips for book signings, group signings, book fairs and other events
- Examples and advice from published authors and marketing experts
- How to track sales on Amazon, including where you sell books

(Continued)

The author began this project to help other authors she published through her company to learn the ins and outs of promoting their new book. The book encompasses all her knowledge and draws from other authors and marketing experts. Learn more at www.bookpromoting101.com.

Easy ordering on Amazon and Kindle.

Contact:
Kristen James
kristen@bravadopublishing.com
Bravado Publishing
541-673-0636

Websites:
www.bookpromoting101.com
www.bravadopublishing.com
www.writerkristenjames.com

Use Your Book to Promote Online

You should have a website set up before your book goes to press so it can include your website address. Before going to press with this book, I launched a blog that features different articles on promoting and shares about me, my other websites and the book.

Next give readers a reason to visit your website. Tell them what valuable things they will find there. Here are a few ideas.

For Fiction
- Discussion guides for reader groups
- The story behind the book
- Monthly contests
- Your blog on writing, publishing or something else that's useful
- Your interviews with other authors, your editor or your agent
- Resources for other aspiring writers
- Information on your book's setting

For Nonfiction
- News about the book's topic
- Worksheets and guides
- Color charts
- The story behind the book
- Additional research
- Updates on the information
- A newsletter

Book Reviews

Local papers are a wonderful resource for authors. You'll find two of my newspaper reviews for *The River People* in the back of this book. Remember to think big and send your new book to the big papers, local papers and book reviewers. Work with your publisher, if you have one, instead of depending on the publisher to get your book out there.

Self publishers have a bigger mountain to climb when it comes to getting reviews. Many book reviewers have a set-in-stone policy against reviewing self published books. They know the public wants to read reviews on really good books, and there is no guarantee a self published book is worth reading. Truthfully, anyone can self publish, and some authors do not edit, proof or format correctly. If your book is one of the good ones, you have to prove this to the reviewers. That's why it helps to have a media kit full of reviews when you send your book to a reviewer. You can gather these from local papers, local librarians and even teachers.

Sometimes when you volunteer, sponsor or otherwise get involved in a school or library program, you can network with librarians and teachers and ask them to review your book.

A Resource for Independent and Self published Authors
Midwest Book Review publishes a list of publications helpful to librarians and readers including:

- *The Bookwatch*
- *Children's Bookwatch*
- *Internet Bookwatch*
- *Library Bookwatch*
- *Reviewer's Bookwatch*
- *Small Press Bookwatch*

You can find information on each of these at
http://www.midwestbookreview.com/index.html.

This page states, **"The Midwest Book Review gives priority consideration to small press publishers, self published authors, and academic presses,"** and offers a link to submission guidelines. They require a cover letter; two copies that are *not* early, advance or otherwise unfinished; and your media kit all mailed to:

James A. Cox
Editor-in-Chief
Midwest Book Review
278 Orchard Drive
Oregon, WI 53575

(Current as of December 2010. Use the link just mentioned to check for updates of editors' names or addresses.)

The entire site is full of informative articles for authors and independent publishers, including a long list of book reviewers used by librarians at
http://www.midwestbookreview.com/bookbiz/advice/bkrevmag.htm.

Resource for Romance Authors
Romance writers can visit www.coffeetimeromance.com, a site that reviews books when you email them a free PDF.

When to Get Reviews

It's very important to know that some reviewers will review only advance copies before publication. Advance reviewers include these publications:

- *Booklist*
- *Library Journal*
- *School Library Journal*
- *Publishers Weekly*

You will want to send them an advance copy three to six months before publication. Traditional publishers do this for most books, and you can always check lists with your publicist to ensure advance copies will go out. Authors who work with a big publisher will still tell you that promotion is your department. Your publisher (if you have a traditional one) will help with promotion, but many times it's up to you. Self published authors are completely in charge of their promotion and need to gather reviews themselves.

It greatly helps a book's launch to have prepublication reviews because you can include them in the finalized copy, so I suggest trying many review sources such as other authors or experts in your book's subject matter.

Other sources can review an advance copy or a finalized copy after publication, such as newspapers and magazines.

Midwest Book Review is an excellent source of reviews and looks only at a finalized copy of the book. Information on these sources is explained in greater detail in the next tip.

Once the book is published, you can continue gathering reviews from newspapers, other authors, experts and readers. You will need the book to be published to receive online reviews on Amazon, Barnes & Noble, Powell's Books, BookaMillion and other similar sites.

The Truth About Reviews

Many of us turn to book reviews in the newspaper, especially the big papers for reviews on big titles.

A book review is a powerful tool for any author. You can post it on your website, later versions of the book and on sales sheets, and you can quote it in all promotions.

Not many people realize how difficult it is to get a good review when they don't have a large publisher, an agent or publicist. It can be difficult to get reviews even with that extra help.

If you're in charge of promoting your own book, here's the truth on getting reviews.

You can't mail your book to a big newspaper and expect a columnist or reviewer to review it. A newspaper columnist in a town of 20,000 people gets free books from the big publishers by requesting them. The newspaper gets 20 pages faxed every day from the big self publishers too. On top of that, authors mail in so many books that the reviewer has a box of them every week.

That makes it hard for you to get attention. So, how do you do it?

Stay local if it's your first book. If you're sending the book out yourself, send it to your local paper, along with a media kit. Begin your letter by stating that you're a local author, and then give the hook, what will really make this book sell.

When you get a review, add it to the media kit so the next reviewer will see it.

When you run into a reporter, a columnist or anyone writing reviews, give that person a copy of your book. Sometimes you make a personal connection when give someone your book. That person might even write a story about it. When promoting, giving away copies results in sales.

Part 3: Your Book Launch

Book Party!

What better way to launch your book into the world than to have a book party?

You can have a lavish party at a rented location. Perhaps catering is in order. This is thinking big! If you've dreamed of this day for a long time, this could be the option for you.

Or you can host a party at your home. Either way, a book-launch party is a wonderful thing for you as an author. Celebrate your hard work!

This party is also a way to let people know your book is out. You can invite the media if the situation is right, invite people who will write about your book and have books on hand to sign and sell. Take pictures and ask people if you can use them on your website and in your promotion.

Party Ideas
- Children's books: Have a daytime party with kids. Read the book.
- Fiction: Read your first chapter or favorite part.
- Nonfiction: Pull out a few tips or facts; read a passage.
- Thank the people who have helped you along the way.
- Hold a raffle for a free copy.
- Record yourself reading or speaking about the book, and use this video on your website.

Hand Selling or Online Promoting?

When authors read this, some quickly assume hand selling their book is much easier than selling online. Another group does not want to get out there to sell their book and would much rather promote via the internet, from the comfort of their computer chair. A third group isn't sure how to promote with either method.

You may well have talent for one area, and I urge you to use your strengths. I also urge you to step out of your normal routine and sell, sell, sell in new and exciting ways. I'll show you how.

If you're better at one form of promoting, you can use the other method to strengthen it. If you love meeting new people and handselling your book, you can direct readers to your website (full of useful information) and your blog all about an interesting topic, and you can use the Internet to tell people about your events.

If you're excited about blogging, online ads, Facebook and tweeting, you can use this to build an online persona. Get out there and meet people online, and then take that energy into the real world at signings, events and conferences. You'll feel more comfortable about greeting people because you've met so many online.

This book aims to show each author how to use your personal talents to reach readers.

Always Carry Copies of Your Book with You!

Why? I met an author in a café to discuss publishing and showed her several different books I had worked on. A man stopped by our table to ask if we were selling the books. Later, another woman stopped by and asked, "Are you the author?" She wanted to buy copies too.

Whenever people learn I'm an author, they ask where they can get my books. It's great to be able to say, "I have some copies in the car!"

Authors tell me their friends will stop them on the street and say, "I heard your book is out. Do you have any with you?" Sometimes, while an author is showing the book to someone she knows, a complete stranger will overhear them and want to buy a copy too. You might be showing your book or books to a friend or someone you just met, and other people will notice. They might even talk to you or buy a book, and even if they don't, they'll remember your name. People get excited to see an author with her book. I've sold books this way, made connections and started conversations. It can be amazing.

So, keep a box of books in your vehicle, and put a few copies in your book bag wherever you go.

When someone asks you what you do for a living or what have you been up to lately, say, "I'm an author. Here's my latest book." Even if you have a day job, make sure to tell people about your book as well.

I've had people stop me because they overheard me talking about one of my books. One nice lady got my business card so she could go online and order a copy. Many people will not go this extra step, so it will pay off if you have copies handy to sell. Keep copies of your book stocked at home too.

Maybe your book just came out in stores, so you think you don't need to sell in person like this. Why not? Even if you carry only one copy to show, you can show off your book and tell people, "It's in bookstores right now."

And one last reason why you should carry several copies of your book: it's plain fun to sell a book this way. Here you are going about your day, and you get to share with someone that you're a published author.

Think Ahead
- Are you involved in any groups where you can show off your book?
- Are you planning any trips? Take your book!
- Do you volunteer anywhere? Or want to? Take your books into a retirement home, a school, a library or church.

Wear Your Book

Great For Children's Authors

I've seen children's authors print up T-shirts that feature the cover or main character from their book. These are great to wear to book signings to attract people's attention or to any kind of kids' event. If you read your book in the school, wear your shirt! People will probably stop and ask you about it, and you get to promote your book.

If you're a children's book author, you can get away with wearing your T-shirt around town, especially when the book first comes out.

One T-shirt will probably run around $10 to $20. If you get more, the cost per shirt may go down. You can print children's sizes and use them as prizes, or maybe your kids or grandkids would like to wear them. Many children's authors are mothers, so you can all wear your shirts to a library event, school event or any other community event. It will be fun when people read it and ask you, "Oh, you wrote a book?"

This is a shirt with the entire cover, which you can order online, a local print shop or use iron-ons. See page 63 for hints on how to print promotion items like these.

This is another idea by children's author Della Neavoll. She had a T-shirt designed from her artwork. The front of the shirt matches the book's front cover, and the backs match up as well. Take a look below. Della sold her books left and right on the street in her community!

Visit Stores, Libraries and Schools

In conjunction with holding book signings and events, make author appearances at stores, libraries, schools and other places where you can promote your book. Libraries and schools like authors to read their book and talk about writing, the story and being an author. Think of these events as "promoting the package" and being a celebrity. Have fun!

Children's authors can really invest in children by visiting and getting them excited about reading, but this isn't just for young children. I had the opportunity to speak to an online group that ranged in ages from middle school though high school. The teacher had ordered books for her class and later left me a review on Amazon. You can use these opportunities to not only connect with readers, but to talk to bookstore owners, librarians and teachers.

If someone invites you to speak or have a book signing, you can rev up your book promotion. Announce it to the media if applicable. These events can get your name out in the community and help you make connections.

Contests and Other Publications

Winning or even placing in a contest is a wonderful way to promote you as a writer and often your book. This depends upon what kind of contest it is. Sometimes you can win money or publication, and it gets you all kinds of free publicity.

If you do well in a contest, you can send out a press release or news tip to papers, email the world about it, add it to your website and blog, and use it as one of your writing credentials.

Short Story Contests

There are countless writing contests out there for different genres and different lengths. Many short story journals also run contests. You can enter the contest and be considered for publication, even if you don't place. *Glimmer Train*, out of Portland, Oregon, is one of the best places to get published for short fiction. You can submit to an open reading or contest. They pay very well for short stories and even better for contests.

If you want to start with something smaller, your writing group might sponsor a writing contest.

I like entering the different *Writer's Digest* writing competitions, which you can read about in *Writer's Digest* magazine and its website. These come with a really nice cash prize, a paid trip to New York and meeting with editors and agents whom you choose. The prizes go to tenth place in most of the contests. The top 25 names are published in a book, and the top 100 are listed on the website.

I placed in the 2009 short story competition in the top 100, and in 2010 I moved up to 32nd place in the young adult and children's fiction category. Of course, I used this in announcements to promote my writing in general and to get people to my website. Both years I wrote a short Native American fiction story, so it works very well for promoting *The River People*. I've had both stories on my website and the Facebook page for *The River People*. If you place with a short story in a contest, you can probably submit it to magazines, journals and other publications and get it published after the contest. (Just make sure to wait until after the contest has published it first.)

Manuscript Contests
Some contests are for unpublished manuscripts. Winning one of these is a good way to get the attention of an agent or editor. Romance Writers of America (RWA) has a manuscript contest for members and another award for published books. I've entered some of these simply because they gave each entrant a critique of their first three chapters. It's nice to get something for your money if you don't win, and good, honest critiques are hard to come by.

Book Awards
There are many contests for newly published books. Your publisher should be able to enter you into some of these, but you will probably need to get the ball rolling. When you're in the editing and polishing stages of any book, think ahead to promotion. Research any contests and awards that you can submit to. The bigger the award or competition, the better it is to win it. This means you might be able to win a small contest, but look for contests and awards with national reach too.

***Writer's Digest* Self Published Books Awards**
This is another huge contest that can generate a lot of attention for your self published book, plus you win $3,000, a paid trip to New York and meetings with agents or editors.

Short Story Publications
Another way to strengthen your writing credentials and gain exposure and publicity is to submit short stories to magazines and journals. Some specialize in flash fiction, longer works, a specific genre like science fiction or maybe just new and experimental works. Get sample copies from publications, or look to the ones you already read.

Whenever you get anything published, use it to promote all your writing work.

Sponsor Something

Schools send kids out to local businesses all the time asking for a small donation to support a school sport, club, event or field trip. Often, the sponsors get an ad on the game program, a listing on a flier or their name on a banner or the team's big picture.

If you can make a small donation to anything like this, you can get your book's cover out there for people to see. This may even be cheaper than a newspaper ad and may put you in a very good light.

You can also volunteer on a planning committee or fundraising event. Look for opportunities that relate to writing, your book's topic or one of your interests. Then be open to sharing about your book.

When you give your time and money to good causes, you're getting involved in your community. Just through meeting people and getting to know them, you'll make more connections that know you're an author.

I found a great opportunity by joining the planning committee for a local book fair. (More on book fairs in a later tip.) I joined because I wanted to see the book fair happen. It would be an exciting opportunity for many local and regional authors and a chance for us to get together and network, along with selling books. Planning the event did take time, effort and a little money, but I did get to spend more time with writers from my area and make some connections. I know more about the other people as writers and as people. I know more about what they write and are interested in; therefore, I'll see possibilities later on for us to help each other or work together.

In the midst of our promoting efforts, the local paper called and asked to interview me about the book fair. (It's a town of 20,000, and the paper is widely read.) The reporter wanted to talk about my own writing and my publishing company because she planned to highlight the two publishers who would be at the book fair. Talk about great press! I was ecstatic to talk to her, and we discussed my favorite topics for an hour and a half. I showed her books I had published by local authors and posed for pictures.

The story came out the Thursday before the book fair and covered my publishing company and another local company with a different specialty. Many people attending the book fair came to talk to me about publishing because they had read the article. Others came because they'd seen my books in the paper while others were just excited to meet all the authors and the two publishers. It was exposure for me and the book fair.

This is an example too of how people can help each other while mutually benefiting and networking. Take a look around your writing community and larger community for chances to get involved, to get out there and to let people know you are an author.

Marketing Books Through Fundraisers for Nonprofits

by B. K. Mayo, author of *Tamara's Child*

Book marketing doesn't always have to mean selling books for profit. You can actually benefit from donating copies of your book to raise money for a good cause. At least that was my experience.

My novel *Tamara's Child* is about a homeless pregnant teenager who is struggling to make a new and better life for herself and her child but who ends up being victimized by the very people she turns to for help. A key scene toward the end of the book takes place at a shelter for pregnant teens. So, it was a natural for me to team up with Safe Haven Maternity Home, a local nonprofit shelter for pregnant teens and teen moms, on a fundraiser for the shelter. I donated 100 copies of my novel to the nonprofit that operates Safe Haven and agreed to provide additional copies for only my printing costs. A number of local, charity-minded businesses agreed to sell the book and turn all the proceeds over to the nonprofit. Sales of the book to date through these local outlets have gone well past the century mark and are still continuing.

So how did I benefit? First of all, it has been hugely rewarding for me personally to know that sales of my book are helping fund this great cause—a cause that I felt connected with even as I was writing my novel and before I had knowledge of the existence of a shelter for pregnant teens in my community. But I also benefited in another way. The fundraiser and my participation in it became front-page news in our local newspaper. The newspaper story, which included a photo of me holding a copy of my novel, helped sell books. Sure, the money raised went to the nonprofit. But the benefit to me in terms of goodwill and publicity for my book was, as the TV commercial says, priceless.

There's no guarantee, of course, that if you donate books to a nonprofit for use in a fundraiser or, perhaps, provide them with books for resale at a greatly discounted price, your efforts on their behalf will become front-page news. But I am willing to bet that the personal satisfaction you receive in supporting a worthy cause related to the subject of your book will be well worth your financial largess. You wrote your book because you have a passion for your subject. Somewhere out there, there's a nonprofit organization that shares that passion. Contacting them regarding using your book as a fundraising sales item can be to your mutual benefit. It can also be a way for you and your book to make a difference in this world. After all, book marketing is not—or shouldn't be—all about selling for profit.

The Library Market

The library market can be very lucrative for the right book. Surprised? I've found myself wondering if selling books to libraries is worthwhile, and then I learned Avalon Books markets exclusively to libraries. It doesn't distribute books to bookstores. The American Library Association states there are 123,000 libraries in the United States, which spend $2 billion on books each year.

If you have a traditional publisher, the publisher should be placing your books into libraries for you, but again, you can market your book too. The library market is a wonderful place for new authors to promote their books. Many authors build a part of their following from readers who found their books in libraries.

Libraries are a source of information for many people, so libraries are very open to nonfiction books. (Tip: that's why your marketing plan and all your promotional material should show how your book helps readers.)

Novels can get into libraries too but have more competition. Help your novel by sending it to library journals for review, such as:

- *BookList* (American Library Association, at www.ala.org)
- *Library Journal* (www.libraryjournal.com)
- *School Library Journal*

Three other big review publications are *Publishers Weekly, Kirkus* and *Foreword Magazine*. I'd advise having several strong reviews from very good sources before sending books to these larger publications. Remember, many of these publications review advance copies before publication.

It also helps to have a local librarian (or one you know, whether or not he's local) review it and send the review out with your book.

Highlight your book's local connection, if it has one. If your book relates to your state's history or culture, feature this in your promotion.

Always include reviews when sending your book for a new review or consideration for purchase.

To find your state's libraries, visit http://www.librarysites.info/. When you click on a state on the U.S. map, it will open a list of that state's libraries. Each name is a link to that library's website. Mailing promotional material to libraries across the United States might not be worth the time and money, but you can target local libraries, which are usually open to local authors.

Library Association Conferences
Handselling to one library at a time, or even to a district, can be time consuming, although sometimes it is rewarding to have your book in local libraries. I've talked about thinking big, and, in this case, thinking big is going to a state library association's conference to market your book. Think of it as a giant book signing, except you are promoting to library book buyers, not just individuals.

This is a link to the American Library Association's list of state chapters:
http://www.ala.org/ala/mgrps/affiliates/chapters/state/stateregional.cfm.

This link provides addresses, contact information and information on each state's conference.

You can join the American Library Association or learn more about it at www.ala.org.

Co-Operative Exhibits and Ads
It can be expensive to rent a booth at a conference or run an ad in a library association publication. However, you might know other authors who would like to work together and share the cost.

Have Someone Else Show Your Book
Along with going directly to the source, you can use distributors who will market your book for you at library conferences, such as Quality Books, http://www.quality-books.com/. (Be sure to include the hyphen in the middle of the address, or you'll end up at a site selling ebooks.)

A company like this will display your book at trade shows and/or include it in their publication and marketing to libraries. They receive a cut of your profit for this service and may also charge upfront fees.

Quality Books appears to have reasonable prices. I've found other companies that charge much more, which is why I mention just this one company. There are other considerations: This kind of company will display your book along with its other paying customers, and it take a big percentage of your book's price when libraries purchase it.

Distributors such as Quality Books often have a mailing program and will market your book through direct mail for you.

Book Signings—Have Them!

Many authors are shy, busy or just don't think a book signing will sell books. You might be afraid you'll end up sitting there by yourself for several hours without selling any books. It takes time. It takes money when you order the books yourself, instead of the bookstore. But you're looking at it the wrong way!

The truth is that book signings are the best way to sell your book.

If your books are in a store, on the shelf, people may not notice them.

Now imagine you are in the front of the store with your books, ready to share them.

This makes a personal connection with people. It motivates them to read your sign, look at the book, remember your name and face or remember the book and buy it if it's in their field of interest.

A book signing shows you believe in the book, and it kicks off your promotion as well as keeps the book in people's minds.

When I was first published, I mailed out a letter about my book to bookstores within a hundred miles. A Barnes & Noble manager called me and said, yes, she would love to host a book signing. It was a busy store in Medford, Oregon, and I was sitting right in front of the main entrance. Because I had traveled for this signing, I actually had not promoted it much. I didn't have a poster or big sign there, so I simply greeted everyone who came in the door.

I sold 17 books in two hours. I sold to a truck driver, a young girl and everyone in between.

What did this teach me? A smile can go a long way. Now I wave people over, smile, stand to talk to them and try to be as welcoming as possible. The book interests people, but I have to get them to come over and look at it.

Location

Bookstores selling used books love to host signings. They'll allow you to post a flier about it for a couple of weeks prior to the event and maybe help you promote it. It's even better if they have a coffee shop or café so people can get refreshments.

Chain stories will sometimes allow self published or print on demand authors to have a signing, and some will even order books through their system for you.

Local businesses usually like having events, so check into cafés, restaurants and even wine-tasting events. I've been involved in a group signing at a local restaurant that was very successful. Diners had their meal and then walked through the authors' room.

Look at locations related to your book's topic:
- The feed and supply store for books on horses, even children's books
- The home and garden store for do-it-yourself books, landscaping, etc.

Do More Than Just a Book Signing

Turn it into an event that offers something to readers. This gives them a reason to stop by besides just buying your book. It's just like people go to your website for information more so than to read how to buy your book.

Speak on your book's nonfiction topic. Explain a few of the tips and hints, or show how the book benefits readers.

Children's authors can read their book, have coloring pages or a simple craft or even a talk about how to write a story.

Fiction novelists can showcase the local slant, the big hook or something about the book that readers will want to know about. If there is a special location in the book, speak about that spot's history or the event in your book.

Book Signings—Tips

- Have a great-looking book. If you self publish, make sure your cover does not look like you designed it yourself in Photoshop, unless you design things for a living or serious hobby. You can purchase great looking artwork and photos from sites such as www.dreamstime.com. You may know a professional illustrator or someone who is trained and very talented. Look to freelancer sites such as www.elance.com and www.guru.com. Run an ad in the paper, check www.Craigslist.com or the Yellow Pages.

- Choose a high traffic location such as a busy bookstore, and ask which days and times the store has the most customers. Many sales come from people who happen into the store/café/location, not from people who saw a flier or know you. This probably changes as you become well know, but don't rely on it in the beginning!

- When you plan your signing, check if the bookstore can order your books. Most can order books through their own book system, for a local author, although Borders and its affiliates have a separate ordering system and often won't order self published books.

- Advertise with attractive fliers, on your website and on Facebook, and ask others to help you spread the word. Try to advertise to the people who will care about reading your book. Send information to schools and libraries for a children's book. Mail a press release to any group that might be interested in your book's topic. Submit information to the paper for the community calendar.

- Have posters of your book cover displayed with you. You can add a review from Amazon or a newspaper to it. Have a flier of reader reviews.

- Don't just sit there all day, unless you need to for health reasons. People will feel more welcomed if you're standing, ready to great them. Of course, I sit down sometimes, but just standing up can get attention. Smile, greet people, ask them to come look at your book. Hand them a copy. This gets people to read the back cover and look inside.

This last tip can make all the difference. If you can find any way to engage people, they will spend time at your table and be more likely to buy your book. Ahead of time, think about how your book helps readers or why they might be interested. Greet people, be excited and tell them about the book.

Here is my display at a book fair. I use an 11 x 17 poster to grab readers' attention. This size is eye-catching, but it doesn't hide me or overwhelm the table. I see people read it as they walk up to me, and then I begin talking to them about my books.

I also place a stack of books out, with two in front. One shows the cover; the other displays the back. I've noticed people don't pick up a book if there are only one or two at the edge of the table.

My business cards are front and center so people can easily take one, and I usually have them inserted in the books too.

Multi Author Signings

Having a book signing with several other authors has big benefits for each involved.

- You're not sitting there alone
- Each author draws in readers who can meet the other authors.
- Each author adds advertising and promoting power.
- Readers might come just because there is a group of authors there.
- Each author can contribute to a raffle prize or gift basket to draw in more people.
- You can have a blast visiting with your author friends and meeting new people, and you leave with a happy literary buzz.
- Advertising posters will look even more attractive because they showcase several authors.

You can utilize this idea by going in with a few other authors to rent a table at an event.

I often see signings with two or more authors who write the same kind of book. Two authors local to me, Bonnie Leon and Ann Shorey, both write Christian romances and have signings together at the bookstore, the mall and book fairs.

Or maybe you want to offer a variety of book genres. However you plan it, it's still like a double or triple feature for readers.

I love multi author signings because you can visit and have a great time, on top of greeting readers and selling books.

The same tips apply: engage readers and be friendly!

Book Fairs—Even Better!

These events can be called an author fair, book fair or book and author fair. I've mentioned joining a planning committee to get one started in my area, and I know of several similar events within my state.

Google to see if you can find any book fairs in your state. It's often not too expensive to rent a table, running around $25. You might be lucky and have a large event already planned in your state.

The benefits are similar to a multi-author signing, on a larger scale:

- You're there with 30, 60 or hundreds of other authors!
- The event will promote it, and each author probably promotes it too.
- Readers come because it's a big event.
- There are usually good raffle prizes, deals or specials.
- You will have a blast visiting with other writers and readers, and you'll float on the buzz for days.
- Authors sell more books at bigger events.
- Authors can network, trade books and learn from each other.

With all of these events, you can take notice of how other authors set up their display table, how they promote and how they sell their books. You also get to network and learn all kinds of exciting things about other authors' writing, their book promotion, their plans, and interesting things they've done as a writer.

Writers often work alone at home so an event like this offers a sense of community, connection, the exchange of ideas and the excitement of being around others that love writing.

Trade Shows and Other Events

If you have a chance to present to libraries, go for it! You can market to libraries at different state library association conferences, and you can find other kinds of trade shows.

What about renting a table at a conference or convention that isn't related to writing?

Yes, you'll have to apply and see if you will even be allowed to do this, but let's go with it for a minute. If you rent a table at a business conference, people can buy your book and read it to relax that night.

You might have a book related to the outdoors, so you rent a table at a sportsman show. This is something you should consider if you write anything related to hunting, fishing, foraging, hiking, camping or the outdoors, even if it's fictional.

At book events, I've seen authors promoting books related to a good cause, such as fighting cancer, putting an end to drunk driving and preserving family history. When you look for events to attend, look outside the literary community, but look specifically for events that will draw your target market.

Another type of highly beneficial event is a literacy event. Schools often have book fairs or family fun nights to promote reading. Communities also have literacy celebrations such as the Celebration of Literacy held in Roseburg, Oregon, every year. You can read more about this event at http://www.celebrationofliteracy.net/.

This event has many activities, including a book fair in the mall where children are invited to do crafts, join story time, swap books and have a good time. This kind of event is perfect for children's authors to participate in.

Promoting Events

So, you've planned a signing or group signing or even a book fair/festival. Maybe you joined one already in existence, but you will still want to help promote it.

Step 1: Set up a website (for big events).
Step 2: Set up a Facebook page and run a targeted ad.
Step 3: Place ads on other websites (author websites) and blogs.
Step 4: Ask involved authors to promote the event.
Step 5: Now start local promoting with fliers, interviews on the radio, a story in newspapers, in community calendars and by word of mouth.

You can create an event on Facebook and invite your Facebook friends to it as well.

This list shows you that online promoting is important, especially if you want people to attend who don't live locally.

You can create a buzz around an event just as you can create a buzz around yourself or your book.

I was on the planning committee for The Douglas County Book and Author Fair and also attended as an author. We enjoyed steady traffic all day due to our promoting efforts. The group used online promoting techniques and also "personal" promoting. Local book store owner Karen Tolley suggested that each person personally tell ten people about the fair and invite them. We each tried to talk to people who would tell others about the fair. We visited schools, got on the radio and some members wrote articles for newspapers about the high number of authors in the area. The paper also wrote an article on the fair and the two attending publishers. We held a raffle every half hour and handed out tickets at the door, which helped us know how many people came through. We noticed most of our visitors had known about the event; they were not people who happened by. This took planning and effort, but the event was a success by many measurements and people are excited about having it again next year.

Learn from Others

In life, you can learn so much from other people in your line of work, people in your areas of interest and people who've been through something you're dealing with right now. Why not reach out to other authors and people in the book industry?

This is another valuable reason to have multi-author signings and book fairs. You can network and discuss writing, publishing and promoting. I think some authors might be intimidated as they look around at other displays. It might appear as if others really know what they're doing, and they won't want to share this information with you. But what do you have to lose? I bet that most authors out there, at any level, will enjoy talking shop with other authors.

- Look at how others set up their displays.
- Watch how they talk to others. Do they get people's attention right away?
- Ask them where they got their ideas.
- Ask about their publisher or distributor.
- Share your ideas and tips with others! Brainstorm!
- Share your stories and listen to theirs.
- Look for possibilities to network more and learn more from each other.

Assume that authors want to share information with other authors. It does not hurt someone's sales to help others market their book. Instead, it provides insights for both of you.

Interviews

I have good news for you. It's easier than ever to get an interview. Radio interviews are a traditional promotion tool that still works today, and now you can get interviewed online as well.

When you have news to share, contact local radio stations. Reach out to many different resources. Often people in the media are looking for interesting people and events to cover on the news.

Getting Online Interviews
I work with many business or marketing people who interview authors. These interviews go onto their website, which they use to constantly offer information to readers. They are happy to promote you. They know you will be sending people to their website or blog to hear the interview; it's a win–win situation.

You might find a group that wants you to speak or a class with a webcam. I was contacted by Connections Academy, an online school, because a class was reading my novel *The River People*, and the teacher wanted me to speak to the class for an hour online.

Nonfiction writers can talk about their book's topic and how it helps people or why people should be aware of the issue. If you wrote a self help book or how-to, you have useful information. This is great for an interview and will attract attention.

Fiction writers are often asked about how they get ideas, about writing, about publishing and about how they got started. You can talk about all these and many more topics related to your book and type of writing, especially if the book is related to an event, a group, a location or something else that makes it unique.

An interview is often not about just your book. You get to talk about it, but just remember that people love information. If you give them new knowledge, they'll be interested in your writing.

Offer a Free Book

There are so many ways to do this, each with its own time and place, and benefits. It's basic promotion to give copies of your book to journalists, bloggers, book reviewers and anyone with a public platform who will get your name and book noticed. This tip is more focused on giving books to readers, which is basic book promotion too. Many authors just don't realize that.

I've discovered that giving away a book is likely to result in sales. The person who receives your book may tell others about it, buy one of your other books, buy more of the book to give away, write a review or help you promote in some other way.

Here are different ways to give your book away to promote it:

- If you are attending a literary event, hold a raffle for a print copy of your book. People can sign up for the raffle with their name and number, or you can even collect email addresses for a newsletter. This method helps you collect readers' names so you can contact them again.

- Place your book in a gift basket that another group or event is raffling off or giving away. This way, your book is a gift that will get your name out there. Sometimes you will be listed as a sponsor or mentioned in the event's promoting.

- Give free copies of your book away to "connectors." These are people who will tell others about your book, write a review, loan the book to interested people and help add to the buzz you are creating for your book. I've given free copies to reporters and bloggers and they often will offer to write a review, mention it in a blog, write a feature story or at least keep me in mind for later contact.

- Give free copies of your book to people in return for a review. You can ask them to write something and give it to you, or ask them to write a review on Amazon or Barnes & Noble websites. To do this, ask in person or email, "I would like to share a free copy of my book with you for a review. Would you be interested?" People who are willing to do this are usually your friends or other authors. Just remember, you don't want a fake 5-star review that says, "This is the best book I've ever read!" That won't help you sell more books.

- Offer a free ebook version of one of your books from your website, usually for a limited time. This is a great promotion that will bring people to your website so they'll see your other work. It gets your name out there. Sometimes people will preview the ebook and then buy a print copy.

Does this work? I've posted many free short stories on my website for readers, and this year I decided to give away the ebook for *A Cowboy for Christmas* for a week. People emailed me about it, and site traffic shot up. At the end of the week, I extended it a few days before removing the free ebook link. A few days later, I checked sales. Guess what? Ebook sales for *A Cowboy for Christmas* had gone up while it was offered for free. Further, so did sales on my other books.

Strange?

Many bands have given away an album. You can Google the topic and find many that have made money this way. Radiohead is just one example. The band put an album on its site with a fill-in-the-box option for payment. People could fill in zero or a price. According to SMO blog, 38 percent decided to pay, giving an average of $6. ($8 in the United States.) Did it make money? Does $2,280,000 sound like very much? Not only did they make money, but millions of people have their music and will tell others about it through blogs, emails and word of mouth.

My promotion helped sales so much that I put the free ebook back up, along with an extended preview of another book. If it works, I say keep doing it. (Although you should always be open to experimenting and improving anything.)

- The site www.goodreads.com allows authors to sign up for a free author profile, and it has a Give-A-Way feature. You select the dates to run the promotion and how many books you will give away. The site promotes it and then gives you names and addresses so you can send the books. (You agree not to keep the address or contact the winner for any other reason.) The winners are encouraged to write a review for the book.

- Announce a give-a-way from your Facebook page or fan page, if people comment. Pick the winner and ask him to email his address to you so you can mail him a signed book.

I've heard old thinking that said, "Never give books away!" The line of thought goes that you put a lot of hard work into them and you should get paid. This is mostly true, but you can generate press by giving a few copies away. It's a way to get your name out there.

Consider this: if you win a prize from the radio or even a raffle, don't you tell your family and friends about it? It's something you might tell people a few years from now, if the prize is good enough.

Now consider if you would like a few happy readers to tell others, "I won a book from that author." They might tell others about you and your books.

A self published author is faced with getting the word out about the book. If you give away 100 copies, you're making a big investment. But imagine if those 100 people generate two sales each. Those readers will in turn tell other people.

Offer a Free Chapter

This is a great way to promote a nonfiction book. Send out an email to everyone you know with the subject: "Free Chapter From My book, How To Tame Your Man" (r whatever your book is called).

Start the email with a very short and attractive description of the book, mainly, how will it help readers? What does it offer them? What makes you an expert on the subject or qualified to write the book?

End the email with a link to your website where people can download the book, or attach a PDF file of the chapter. (Some people will not open attachments, so you may want to offer both.)

This is similar to giving away a book, but it works more directly to interest readers in the given book, not your writing in general.

Many authors will blog about a chapter of their book and provide a link to their website. Here people can download the chapter and maybe buy the book.

You can use this idea by writing an article about your book topic and sell it or give it to other bloggers, websites and online sources that will post it. This sets you up as an expert and gets people to come to your website where they can preview your book.

For nonfiction books, you can post the table of contents on the website and share it in emails as well. This is similar to giving away a chapter, but it shows what the book is all about.

Yet another way to give away a chapter is to put your book on Kindle, which allows any Kindle owner to preview the first chapter. Kindle is so great. I'll write about it for my next tip!

Use the Internet, Luke

The plain and simple truth is that if you ignore the Internet, you are ignoring a vast field of advertising and promoting avenues.

You can reach people online who:
- Don't read your local paper
- Don't visit any local bookstores
- Don't visit bookstores at all
- You will never see in person

People go online and search for specific things. A newspaper ad has a limited audience, and many people who see that ad may not read that kind of book. However, if someone searches online for a fantasy novel about mermaids, she'll get a list of every fantasy mermaid book.

Someone might find your blog about raising rabbits and see that you wrote a book on the subject. Another person will read an article you wrote on developing characters and want to read the book mentioned in your bio. A third person might hear your name or see you mentioned somewhere and Google you, find your website and read about your books.

You can use your email to send out information about your books, as well as Facebook, Goodreads, LinkedIn and many other sites. The internet can be a fun way to connect with readers, other writers and interesting people, and you can do this for very little cost.

You can use the Internet to different degrees, from:
- Simply having an email so readers can contact you (You don't have to give your phone number this way.)
- Having a company set up and maintain a website for you
- Using email and Facebook to stay in touch with readers
- Blogging (more on this subject later)
- Setting up your own website, using networking sites

There are many opportunities to use the internet to the degree you are comfortable with.

Online Networking: Part 1

Don't run away! This is easier than it seems. Do you email? You can send an email to everyone in your address book of saved email addresses.

Use this format, which can also work as a press release. First, create a one-page write-up about your book. It should describe the basic story idea and interesting facts about you.

Next, insert a link to your website and your book's page on Amazon. Then ask people to please share this email with others.

There, you have reached out online.

Ask your family members to forward your email and help you promote your book.

If you belong to a writing group, or any group for that matter, ask if someone can send your page to members.

Your next steps are getting a website and then joining sites like www.facebook.com, which we'll cover soon enough.

Online Networking: Part 2

If you're online and emailing, you're ready to join social networking sites.

To join www.Facebook, you simply enter your name, email and birthdate. This last item is to ensure children are not signing up. You can use your page to post news about your book, writing and your life, if it's not *too* personal. Of course, you'll have to send friend requests to people you know.

The site www.LinkedIn.com is a site for professionals to network, and there are many writing groups on this site.

The site www.Goodreads.com is a site for readers and authors to mingle, share about books they are reading and make friends.

I meet many authors who are wary of joining these sites, and for good reasons such as:
- Is your information safe?
- Can someone steal your identity?
- What if you can't keep up with the technology?

Online safety is very important, and you can have online profiles without sharing personal information. You should not display your home address and phone number or ever post that you're on vacation. (Thieves watch for this; beware!) Not many people know this, but you shouldn't display your hometown, where you were born. Identity thieves use this information.

Being safe online is all about being aware and not sharing personal or secure information with anyone. Beyond that, you're ready to network and tell people about your book. You can blog from many of these sites and offer writing tips, describe the writing life and write about your journey as a writer.

Facebook (Using and Marketing)

Okay, I've been talking about Facebook all through this book. Now I will discuss how to actually set up a profile and use the site. If you're already on Facebook, still skim through to the tips that come after setting up a profile.

Are you on Facebook?
When it comes to online networking, there's a group of people who can't wait to log on and connect. Another group doesn't know where to begin. Should you use Facebook? Well, read these statistics from Facebook's site, and then decide:

- More than 500 million active users are on Facebook.
- About 50 percent of active users log on to Facebook on any given day.
- The average user has 130 friends.
- People spend more than 700 billion minutes per month on Facebook.

(This information is from the site in December 2010. You can find updates to this information at http://www.facebook.com/press.)

Just a quick disclaimer: I'm not affiliated with Facebook in any way and am providing this information from the company's website and my own experience.

You can register for free in under a minute at www.facebook.com. You sign up and then begin building your page, which can be very simple. Upload a profile picture and fill in some basic info, and you're good to go. The site is easy to use and guides you through the process. Friends and family can also show you how they upload pictures and find friends online.

You can then create a free page for your book, OR you can go to Facebook and create a page for your book WITHOUT joining, at http://www.facebook.com/pages/learn.php.

Again, this link takes you to a web page that will guide you in setting up a page for your book.

For your book's page, upload your book cover, and fill in its description under "info." There are many ways to use both your profile and book page to connect with readers and grow your reader base.

Having a page for your book allows you to:
- Send out updates on your book
- Offer previews
- Share links
- Share sales
- Give away books
- Share pictures related to your book and topic
- Talk to readers
- Promote with ads

You can also do this from your profile. However, I have a private profile and a public page for my book that anyone can see.

Once your page has more than 25 members, or "likes," you can create a unique URL (website address for it) at http://www.facebook.com/username/.

You can find a page for my historical Native American novel at www.facebook.com/TheRiverPeople. I have a book description, pictures, short stories, a preview and links to purchase the book. I also post interesting facts on Native culture and provide links to other websites. Sometimes I post stories or updates related to my writing in general, not just *The River People*. The page is a community page that anyone can "like" and then post on.

You can also set up a fan page for yourself to promote all your writing. The process is the same as setting up other pages, but just choose the Fan Page option.

Networking
You can network in many ways, such as adding people you know using your email, telling people you're on Facebook, joining groups, checking your friends "friends list" and searching for people. Facebook has a "friend finder" to guide you.

Your website should say you're on Facebook and provide a link, and your Facebook page should list your website. If you have an author website, do book signings or promote other ways, tell people you're on Facebook. Many will look for you if they're on the site as well.

If you're new to Facebook, these instructions might sound complicated, but the site is really easy to use.

Using Facebook Ads (a paid service)
Facebook allows you to create an ad that will link to the Facebook page or your website. It will have you type the text, upload a picture, insert a link by typing in the web address (or copy and paste) and then enter payment information.

The ad will show to users on Facebook, according to the demographics that you choose: men, women, romance readers, people who like history and so on. Customize this to your book's topic.

You set a daily budget of how much you want to pay each day. That means you might be charged up to this amount if people click on your add. You also pick how much you are willing to pay for each click. So, you can set a daily budget of $5, and say you will only pay 95 cents per click. It's a bidding system. If you're launching a new book, you might want to set your daily budget and click Bid Higher. It all depends on how much you want to spend.

Another Lesson from Facebook
It's just mind boggling to think about the site's size and the number of users on Facebook. It's snowballing out of control—in a good way. But there is an interesting lesson for anyone who really pays attention. This site has more than 500 million users, yet Facebook promotes itself on Facebook, Twitter and its own blog. If Facebook is promoting for more users, how can we think we shouldn't promote for more readers?

Blogging

To blog or not to blog? Well, you can blog for free, so it's a good place to begin you online adventures if you are new to emailing and "Facebooking." A blog is an open conversation with the world.

You can have a blog to share your thoughts with the family and friends who know about it, and see if it grows. You can also advertise it and share the link while promoting your book or books.

Some people are excited to blog, whereas others aren't sure what it is, if it will take too much time or if anyone will actually read it. Blogging has a time and place.

Blogging is a great promotional tool for a nonfiction writer. Imagine you wrote a book about dog training, and you blog about dogs, training, keeping them healthy and funny dog stories. You are offering free information free, and it promotes your book.

You can blog about your book's topic if you wrote a self-help book, how-to, relationship guide or any topic that lends itself to discussion.

If you wrote a parenting book, you can blog about children, fun times, tips and recipes, and ask readers to post their thoughts.

Many fiction writers employ blogs as well to keep readers updated, to write about writing, to share story excerpts and short stories, to blog about the journey of getting published or possibly on a completely different topic.

If you've been writing awhile, you can share writing tips and links to articles and other blogs that you find helpful. A blog can serve as an information hub about your topic. When you share free information with readers, it puts you in a good light and gives them another reason to pick up your book.

Look at www.blogspot.com and www.wordpress.com to see how to set up a free blogs or Google "Free blog" for other options.

Group Blog

Avalon Books hosts a group blog for all its authors. Many have their own blog and website as well, but this group blog is a place where they make posts about writing, publishing, their books, author interviews and just stuff about life.

A group blog offers exponential advertising and promotion. Each author probably has a link or two going to the blog and advertises it. The publisher advertises it, and readers will visit because they read one of the authors. This gets exposure for the other authors as well.

A group blog can offer a wide range of expertise and knowledge, along with letting readers get to know a bit about each author.

Each author can have a bio on the blog that talks about her books and provides a link back to the author's website. It can be a great promotional tool.

Does your writing group have a blog? Maybe it's time to start one. Blogs and websites do not have to be either/or. An author or group can have a website, a blog and a Facebook page, along with profiles on other sites.

Having a blog in addition to a website is nice because it's very easy to post a new article or blog post to your blog. It allows people to comment and interact with you too.

Promote with Articles
Article Marketing

A simple way to promote your writing with articles is to submit them for publication to paying newspapers and magazines. This gets your name out there, but it usually doesn't provide online links to your website.

If you want your articles to promote your website and book more directly, give away articles to online sources.

How?

For nonfiction books: write and give away an article based on a chapter in your book. Give this to people with websites that get heavy traffic—marketing websites, blogs related to your topic and places where the article will help people. Because you're giving the article away (giving people more useful information for their website, helping them), you should have a link in the article or at the end. This link will go to your website where you can offer that chapter for free.

You can set it up so that people receive this chapter only if they sign up for your newsletter or subscribe to your blog. Or you can just provide a link if you want to keep things simple. This free chapter will entice readers into buying the book. Make sure your free chapter includes reviews for the book and links or information about where they can buy it.

For novelists: give away articles on writing, how you get inspired or something useful you can offer about the publishing industry. The key is giving away useful information or insights that readers will want to know.

If you network with people in the industry, other authors and blog writers, you probably know people who will be happy to post your guest blog or article.

Content Is King

ou take away one lesson about the Internet from this book, remember this:

The internet is an information and content war.

This is useful for anyone who is looking for specific information. Yet, this makes it a bit hard to draw traffic into your site.

A solution is to offer good information on a regular basis. Update your website and blog with information that visitors will want to read. If you advertise your books constantly, just trying to make a sell, you will make less sales!

The websites and blogs with the most useful information get the most online traffic. You want to offer more than just a sales pitch for your book. Give people a reason to come to your website or blog, and give them reasons to return.

Google all your favorite authors, and look over their websites and blogs. Often you'll find an interesting bio, writing tips, resources for writers, tour dates, links, blogs about getting an agent, the publishing process, what the writer is dealing with during revisions and reviews.

I came across many very useful blogs and websites whiles researching promoting, and one in particular called The Creative Penn. It offers monthly ezines, a constant supply of articles on writing, publishing and promoting, and the blogger is very active on her blog. If you comment, she'll often comment back the same day. It's a giant information hub for authors. I bookmarked it on my computer to return and "liked" her Facebook page, and I plan to read her new articles.

People love to learn, and the Internet makes it possible to goggle any subject for instant learning. If you don't offer new and useful information, along with your books, you'll lose readers to better sites.

Kindle

Publishing to Amazon's Kindle is so easy; you merely upload a Word document! Visit https://kdp.amazon.com/self-publishing/signin to create an account and put in some information. Then you can begin uploading files to publish to Kindle.

Kindle owners already spent around $150 to have the Kindle, so I believe they are more apt to buy more books and try new authors. Money is less of an issue, and they don't have books lying around if they buy ten a day. They can purchase and download a book with one click, making it very, very easy to buy a book.

I've read that Kindle owners buy three times as many books as paper readers do. In the online discussion boards I visit, I've seen comments like:

- I won't buy a book unless it's on Kindle.
- I'm seeing impaired, and Kindle has opened reading to me again.
- I'll buy short stories and collections on Kindle.
- I'll try new authors.
- I'll browse the Kindle store and read reviews for new books to read.
- I'm handicapped, and downloading ebooks makes it possible for me to get more new books.

Kindle readers are book lovers to the core, and they are searching the Kindle store for new books to read.

Kindle is a great tool for you as an author because you are in control and can see sales reported at the end of each week.

By publishing your book through print and ebook forms, you are reaching a much wider audience.

Author Central on Amazon

This is a sharp tool for your author's tool belt. As soon as you have a book on Amazon, you can sign up for an author's account. This is true for self published authors and traditionally published authors alike. Do not miss out on this wonderful way to connect with readers and track sales.

https://authorcentral.amazon.com

When logged in, you can see tabs across the top of your screen: Home, Books, Profile, Videos, Events, Blog, Sales Info and Reviews. (Nice, huh? Now you can go to a one-stop location to view all kind of information that will help you target your marketing!)

After you sign up, you can add an author bio and your books. You will soon have a page listing you and your books, and you can log into Author Central to:

- Updates books
- Update your author bio
- Upload several pictures of yourself
- Blog
- Track where your book is selling under the Sales info tab

The Sales Info tab starts with a tour explaining how to use it and then shows you a map of the United States. You can see highlighted states where you've sold books, graphs of sales and your Amazon bestseller ranking for each title.

These resources are just plain fun too. This week I sold books in South Carolina, two place in Texas, California, Florida and Arizona. This shows my online marketing and that word of mouth is working so that people across the United States know about my books.

Reader Reviews on Amazon

It's a great thing when a reader reviews your book on Amazon, Barnes & Noble or any other site selling it. There is one tiny catch: if it's obvious that your best friend wrote it, and says it's the best book ever, people won't believe it. You need to go about getting honest reviews for your book.

It's fine to give people a copy of your book and ask them to review it online. It's even better when a reader out there likes your book so much that she reviews it.

When you get reader reviews, use them. Don't just let them sit there, even though this will help your book sales. Utilize them to the max. If you receive a few new reviews, post an update on Facebook, Myspace and other sites you use, and include a link to the Amazon page with the review. Copy and paste these reviews onto your website and promotional materials.

If someone you know posts a review for your book, make sure to thank that person. Many people just don't feel comfortable posting reviews, so it can take some work and time for an author to get very many.

Backlist and Why It's So Great

I've seen many authors publish a new book and leave the old ones in the dust. (Picture the dusty bookshelf.)

It's fine and dandy to promote your newest release, and you should promote like the wind. Just don't neglect the money you can make on your old books.

Why is this so great?

The book is produced and published. You have no new costs to recover. It's all profit, baby. If you promote an older book and it sells, you're making residual income. You have money coming in for something you did five years ago. Hooray!

Promoting your backlist is as easy as promoting yourself. You promote your writing, right? You meet people who like your present book, and you can tell them about other books you think will interest them.

My first published novel, *The River People*, has the broadest audience. As a historical book, it's not tied to any event. In that sense, it's like a classic. I've been promoting it from the start and see royalties come in all the time.

If you have five books published, just think of the possible income. Even if they aren't bringing in thousands on their own, they can add a nice sum to your income.

Your backlist also shows readers you're a career author, not a one-hit wonder. It shows your commitment and love of writing.

If you have books out there that aren't selling, read through these tips, and write a promotion plan to relaunch those books.

Book Tours

If that sounds like an expensive idea to you, that's because it is. Well-known authors can go on a book tour, and readers will come out to meet them and buy books. Readers don't, however, make a point of going to a book signing by an out-of-town author they haven't heard of before, or one they don't know much about. So, what do you do?

Well, you don't want to give up on this kind of promoting, but there is a better way.

Instead of spending money on traveling across your state or region, why not take a look at the trips you would normally take that year? Do you visit kids, grandkids, friends or relatives across your state or the country? All of your trips can have a double purpose. Imagine you often visit your brother Nick in the next state over. This year, plan several book signings at your stops or your destination if you're flying. Your brother (or whoever you are visiting) can help promote the signing ahead of time by handing out fliers, announcing it in the paper and letting different groups know about it. You can research and contact any writing or literary groups there.

This idea works many ways. You can reroute some of your normal trips or plan to visit people you haven't seen in awhile. Maybe you can plan a book tour based on where you know people.

Author Beware

If you self publish your book, you will receive and find offers that promise to promote your book for you. One such company contacted my publishing company with an offer to place books in three stores for me, with a growing list of stores that would consider placing the book. This sounded like something I could offer my authors, so I asked for more information. Within an hour, I got a high-pressure phone call. The fee was $1,000. No, that's not a typo. The fee was really one thousand dollars to place one book into three stores. This offer didn't promise to put the book into a chain like Barnes & Noble. It could very well be three bookstores that sell used books near the company offering this.

I get other offers in my email all the time. Some companies offer to market my book to libraries. Because I work in the industry, I'm fairly sure they send out a catalog of book info to different libraries. For even more money, they'll highlight your book at a trade show, meaning you can actually get some exposure. Just be wary of spending way more money than you can recoup.

There are many, many ways to advertise your book to the right audience for less. You can buy an ad in a related magazine or journal and know potential readers will see it. Targeted Facebook ads are much cheaper, and you can even set your daily budget limit. You can sign up and have a table at a trade show and display your own book or books. This book shares many low cost and even free ways to get exposure for your book. If you elect to invest in a marketing program, look for reviews and recommendations online, not the company's own site. Check and see if they can show you books that did well because they were involved in the program.

With this last tip, I want to wish you success with your book!

Part 4: The New Publishing World

No, we're not in Kansas anymore. These days, anyone can put together 50,000 plus words and publish them in book form.

This is good because you and I can publish our books. This is bad because it's harder to find the gems in all the paper.

The Changing Publishing Industry

So, let me explain how things have changed in more detail. In years past, authors wrote books and mailed a query letter out to one publisher at a time. The publisher would possibly request a few chapters and then the entire manuscript. (More and more publishers accept simultaneous queries, meaning you submit to several publishers that publish books like yours.) The author might eventually sell the manuscript and end up with a book in stores. This usually meant an advance and royalties later on. Not as many people could be published authors because the publishers accepted books that would only make a profit.

The Way it Was—and Still is to Some Degree
In this first stage, books were printed in large print runs through a printing process called offset printing, which is still used today in many circumstances. This is the method most people think about when we discuss publishing, and it was the information I learned back in the 1990s when I first learned about publishing. You're probably somewhat familiar with the old model.

Moving Forward
The next phase involved the traditional publishers and large self publishing companies that allowed authors to pay them to publish their book. It cost thousands of dollars even before authors ordered their books in piles of several thousand copies, using offset printing at first. The publishers made a pretty penny. A few of the authors made it huge

because they promoted like their life depended on it. Many others ended up with a garage full of books, due to the required large print run. This enabled more people to be published authors, but the upfront cost was high, and the authors had to handsell their books.

Whenever new technology comes along, it's expensive for a while, and then people figure out how to lower the cost. The first self publishers charged a lot of money, but they also had to use the offset printing that cost more. It opened the door for people to look for better and cheaper ways to publish books.

Today's Publishers

The third phase is where we are now. Along with the big traditional publishers and small independent presses that buy books' rights, there are many different kinds of self publishers. The big self publishers are still here, and they still charge quite a bit to design a book. After that, there is a wide spectrum of fees associated with self publishing, which depend upon how much of the work you do yourself and which publisher you go with.

All publishers today use print on demand (POD) technology to some extent. This process can print one book at a time or thousands, depending upon how many you need. Even Random House uses POD when sales spike and they don't have enough books.

Print on demand is new and different in that it uses a digital computer file and prints much like you do at home.

As you can imagine, this opens a world of possibilities for large publishers, small independent presses and different kinds of self publishers.

POD Publishers

Many publishers are called POD printers or publishers because they use POD as their primary means of publishing. Self publishers rely on POD so authors can print 1, 5, 10 or 100 books at a time.

I use POD for Bravado Publishing so I won't have any inventory to stock or ship out. I don't have to carry the balance while waiting to sell the books. I simply print a book when someone orders it.

You'll hear some books called POD, and this is often synonymous with self published. Almost all self published books are POD, unless an author buys a huge print run of her book. I have the capability to print a large print run, but I have not seen the need with a self published book. It seems risky to handle all the inventory when you can simply print copies when needed, just as you can run copies off your computer.

Some POD publishers are smaller self publishers, like my own company. I charge much less to design a book and publish it online. (I try to help authors get into print at a price they can recoup.) This fee is for the publisher's time, the ISBN and online listings. This is a good publishing method for people who do not want to mess with interior book design, cover design, getting an ISBN and formatting.

There is another kind of self publisher that is more of an automated system, such as Lulu or CreateSpace. These publishers allow you to design and upload your book yourself, often for free. They don't need to charge for their time because you do the work. They usually publish your book to their site, or their site plus Amazon's amazing catchall system. If you can design your own book, this is a good way to self publish. These publishers do offer additional designing services, usually at high price. I researched and found cover design for $299 up to $1,400.

What Exactly Is POD Again?

I know POD can be very confusing to some people. The picture most Americans have about how the publishing industry works is based on how it used to work. I run into so many people who have no idea what POD is, how it works and what it means to authors.

With the print on demand method, books are put into an automated online system. They then appear on every bookseller site online. There is no inventory. The book is not sitting in a warehouse anywhere. The information is available for any online retailer to list.

This seems to be a vague, mysterious and confusing reality to most of the people I talk with. I tell them I publish books online. I explain that no, there is no printing press. I have never put a book together by hand. I don't print them up myself and mail them out. I design a book and put it into a system, and it's printed when someone out there in cyber space orders one.

I have authors call me when we first publish their book. They want to know where the book will appear. I understand where they're coming from. If you have another product, you want to know where it's warehoused and who has it. This is completely different. You see, all sites online can list your book at no cost to them. They let the system supply the information, it shows up on their system without any effort on their part and then they get a cut if it sells through their site.

(Sorry if you're hearing the theme song from *The Twilight Zone*; it should pass soon.)

Your book is listed everywhere, no matter who published it. This means bestsellers, midlist books and self published authors are on Amazon together.

When people order a print on demand book, it's printed and the royalty goes back to the publisher and then to the author. The print fee is taken out of the retail price of the book.

How Do Royalties Work with POD?

Imagine you build dollhouses for a hobby. People see your product in the paper, call you and order one. They pay for it, and you use this money to build the dollhouse. You keep the profit. That's the idea here with print on demand. The buyer pays for the book printing, and the profit comes back to you, the author.

One More Publishing Advance: Ebooks

A large and quickly growing market is ebooks. Readers can purchase and download ebooks to the computer, Kindle readers, Adobe readers, iPhones and several other devices. There is no inventory because books are never printed.

Ebooks are booming right now for many reasons:
- People love technology.
- It's just one click to buy an ebook.
- There are no books lying around the house.
- You can purchase them and store them for later reading.
- You can take 100 books with you everywhere and get new ones instantly.
- The ebook version is even cheaper to buy.

Ebooks are nice to authors and publishers because:
- Ebook readers buy three times are many books as normal, paper book readers do.
- We can have our book in print and ebook form to reach two markets.
- There is hardly any additional work to set up an ebook for your book.

What Does This Boil Down To?

With Amazon, POD and ebooks, we have books, books and more books to choose from online.

There are many fewer books in bookstores but still a lot of competition.

That's why it's important—STILL—to write the best possible book you can and then promote it.

Publishing today is very different, changing and growing, and offering more and more opportunities for authors and readers alike. The playing field has gotten much bigger, allowing in more players, and authors play on this field as both writers and promoters.

Part 5: Success Stories and Author Resources

There are many levels of success in life and in being an author. As you build upon your success, I hope you will also celebrate and enjoy each step. Celebrate new reviews, reader comments and milestones in your writing career.

I feel successful because I make a living from writing and publishing. Having published novels has helped me land ghostwriting or freelance work, which in turn further sharpened my writing skills.

Every author begins with a different dream. Some want a published book to share with people they know while others dream of seeing their name on the bestseller lists. Your dreams are up to you!

Things to consider:

- Money is but one measurement of your book's success.

- Imagine if your book changes the life of others. Even if you change the world for one person, that is success.

- If you sell 1,000 copies of a self help or how-to book, that's 1,000 plus people you have helped. Imagine if you sell 5,000 copies. Books are usually resold or shared, so the true number might be double that.

- The book you wrote for younger readers may be one that sticks with them all their life. That is strong motivation to get your book out to readers.

- Your book can open doors for you to meet new people and influence others. (Volunteer to speak to classrooms, book clubs and groups. It's very rewarding.)

- Promoting will help more people learn about your book and be touched by your story, message, information or guidance. Some topics have a large audience; others have smaller ones.

- Early and continuous promotion is important, and good books often grow a readership for years to come.

One of the biggest joys as an author is sharing a story and a world with other people across the country and world. I enjoy hearing people talk about my books, ask questions and give me feedback. They are not only entertained for a while but also educated about my view of the world or get a look into the past if they read my historical novel. When I listen to others talk about my stories, it seems the characters are lifelike to them too.

This is a feeling many craftsmen share. When you bake the perfect Italian lasagna or batch of white chocolate macadamia nut cookies, you want others there to share and experience with you. Painters create so others can view and appreciate their work. Artistic endeavors are made to enrich the lives of others.

Success Stories

Using the promoting methods in this book has opened many opportunities for me to reach readers across America and even other countries. If *Book Promoting 101* helps you reach your goals, I'd love to hear about it. Maybe I can feature you in the next edition! The following stories are authors who successfully promoted their books with big results.

From Kindle Ebook Sales to Book Deal

Self-Publishing Review online shared about an author's success based on his book's Kindle sales. There's been times when a self published author proved a book's merit through sales and then sold the rights to a large publisher, but this instance may very well be the first time ebook sales have landed a book deal.

Author Boyd Morrison had an agent, but they could not sell his novel, *The Ark*. In the meantime, Morrison uploaded his book to Amazon Kindle and began promoting. He participated in online discussions pertaining to fiction and Kindle, but he didn't simply post ads and leave. Morrison made sure he was contributing to the discussion. (It can really annoy people if you use online forums to promote your book without getting involved and making relevant comments.)

He priced his novel under $2, thinking that readers would be willing to take a chance on an unknown if the book was inexpensive. He was right. People bought the book and told others. Soon more and more people were hearing about his book. Soon, his agent went back to publishers and, because the book was selling so well on Kindle, he got a two-book deal with Simon & Schuster. Nice!

There are a few other factors in his success. Boyd Morrison had blurbs from best-selling authors James Rollins and Douglas Preston. He had met them years before at a Thrillerfest conference. This is how networking can really help you!

This author understood how to promote online, and he knew it would hurt him to blast the Internet with ads. He just participated in discussions.

The other advice he gave was to ensure you have a professional book cover and a well-written description. It goes without saying you need a well-written book that tells a great story. When you have these, promoting and word of mouth will often push sales.

(Source of information on Boyd Morrison: "A Kindle Success Story: How to Promote a Kindle Ebook" by Henry Baum, The Self-Publishing Review. July 14, 2009.)

Other authors are using ebooks sales to prove their book can sell. Karen McQuestion published her books to Kindle and then sold five to Amazon Encore. (Did you miss that? Five book deals!) Check out her books at http://www.karenmcquestion.com/.

Still others are marketing their Kindle books just to make profit on their own. The ebook *Draculas*—written by Blake Crouch, Joe Konrath, Jeff Strand and F. Paul Wilson—rose to No. 76 in the Paid Kindle store on its first day and received 120 reviews that day. I'd bet these four authors worked together on promotion, asking fans to post reviews and blog about their book. Joe Konrath was nice enough to explain their promotion strategy on his blog at
http://jakonrath.blogspot.com/2010/10/live-undead-marketing-draculas.html.

When Your Publisher Doesn't Come Through

Many newly published authors discover that their publisher is busy promoting the sure bets and big names. That's just how the industry works now. On September 24, 2009, the *Washington Post* reported on a new author named Kelly Corrigan who found herself in this spot with her new memoir *The Middle Place*. Other authors were sent on tours and to the National Book Festival, whereas her book wasn't even reviewed by any major newspapers.

Taking matters into her own hands, she created a video book trailer on her computer, using a free music download as background music. Corrigan posted the video on her website. Then her agent got her an interview on a morning show. She didn't stop there. When many of her friends decided to host book parties for her, she went on a tour that she paid for herself. The *Washington Post* article says she sold books from the trunk of her car. At one stop, a friend recorded her reading an essay and posted it on Utube. (Anyone can record and upload videos here to share with the public and then post links to the video or use code to embed the video in other websites.)

Did all this time and money invested pay off? Within a year, her book trailer had been viewed more than 100,000 times. The Utube video had been viewed 4.5 million times. *The Middle Place* spent 20 weeks on the *New York Times* bestseller list!

Book trailers are a new trend and one that can make a huge impact on your success, and it's available to traditionally published and self published authors. These are like movie trailers, ranging from very short 20-second clips to several minutes long

Kelly Corrigan used a short video and the help of friends to jump-start her sales, which shows how creativity can be the thing to tip your book.

Resources

Useful Books

Writer's Market (yearly editions, along with different versions for different genres)

This yearly book is filled with submission guidelines for publishers and agents. It also has a query-letter clinic and other very helpful articles in the front. The query-letter clinic points out what to do and what to avoid. Because query letters contain a short, attractive description of your book, this also teaches you how to write an elevator speech and back cover blurb.

Writer's Market also has a magazine (*Writer's Digest*) and website. Once a year it publishes a list of the best websites for writers in the magazine and the website.

Books on Writing (These are my "keeper" books that taught me how to write.)

The Complete Writer's Guide to Heroes and Heroines
by Tami D Cowden, Caro LaFever and Sue Viders
This book describes eight main character types for both men and women, provides a section describing them and cites famous fictional examples and then shows how each combination interacts. Romance writers, read this book!

GMC: Goal, Motivation & Conflict: The Building Blocks of Good Fiction
By Debra Dixon
This book will teach you how to set up your character's goals, motivation and conflict in chart form. These are the backbone to a good novel.

Creating Character Emotions
By Ann Hood
Hood shows you how to skillfully show emotions in your writing.

Dynamic Characters
By Nancy Kress
Want to create quirky, memorable characters? This book shows how to use many different aspects to craft a lifelike character that people will remember and identify with.

Books on Creative Thinking

A Whack on the Side of The Head: How You Can Be More Creative
by Roger von Oech
A book about creative thinking and ways to look at everything differently.

Tipping Point
by Malcolm Gladwell
What makes a product tip? This book includes information on self published authors who made it big.

Outlairs
by Malcolm Gladwell
What makes some people extravagantly successful? This book defines the story behind "overnight" success with stories of different people. It's very interesting because Gladwell looks at authors too. The sudden success is often the result of the time they spent learning their craft.

Websites

Midwest Book Review: www.midwestbookreview.com/index.html

Book Review: www.bookreview.com

Self Publishing Review: www.selfpublishingreview.com

Complete Review: www.complete-review.com

Once Written: www.oncewritten.com — Book Reviews

My Shelf: www.myshelf.com — Book Reviews

Amazon Author Central: www.authorcentral.amazon.com
Track your sales, see your reviews and update your Amazon profile

Contact Any Celebrity: www.contactanycelebrity.com
Might be useful to get celebrity endorsements

Writer's Digest: www.writersdigest.com

Writer's Digest, 101 Best Sites:
www.writersdigest.com/101BestSites/

Creative Penn: www.thecreativepenn.com

Blogger: www.blogspot.com — Set up a free blog.

Fiction Factor: www.fictionfactor.com — High-quality articles for fiction authors.

Selling Books: www.sellingbooks.com — Full of very practical articles.

Yahoo: www.yahoo.com — Create an email account, purchase web hosting for a website.

Vistaprint: www.vistaprint.com — Print promotional material for very affordable prices.

American Library Association: www.ala.org

Library Journal: www.libraryjournal.com

Kindle: https://kdp.amazon.com/self-publishing/signin — To set up an account.

Index

About The Author

Kristen James works as a full time author, freelance/ghostwriter, editor and book publisher. She lives on the river and enjoys the outdoors like most Oregonians do. A few of her hobbies include reading, cycling, fishing and camping. Lem and Kristen are a modern "Brady Bunch" with six kids, so many of their activities are group activities!

Learn more at about Kristen and her writing at www.writerkristenjames.com.

Learn more about Bravado Publishing at www.bravadopublishing.com. The site details her writing, editing, formatting and publishing services.

Praise for *The River People*

The Herald and News of Klamath Falls called *The River People* "A nicely told tale that discusses American Indians from a different perspective. It combines history with romance, with a hint of early women's liberation, and a larger dose of Indian culture."

From a teacher:
The River People is a great book! It is historical fiction that is fun to read. By following the main characters you learn about life as a Native American in Oregon near the Umpqua River. The characters are strong, especially River-Song, who does not follow the crowd. She breaks from conventional female roles as she tries to choose between one of the most desirable men, Walks-with-Pumas, and leading her tribe after

her father, the chief, steps down. The writing is very readable and enjoyable. I would highly recommend this book and as a parent, teacher, and avid reader.

Review by Tricia Dias of the Douglas County News:
The characters are well developed; the reader cares about them and what's going to happen next. River-Song is a complex person, as all 15 year olds are. However, in her culture, she is no longer considered a child and one day will become the leader of her village. During this critical summer, she leaves the last trace of childhood firmly behind and gains a maturity that stands her in good stead as she faces many challenges, both within herself and from the outside. What direction should she lead her people? How will she meet the threat to her happiness and to her people as a whole? The answers are cleverly woven into a good read.

From author B. K. Mayo:
I love the names of the characters in this historical novel about life among the Native Americans of the Pacific Northwest before their way of life was dramatically altered by the arrival of white settlers in the region. River-Song, the 15-year-old daughter of aging Village Chief Sits-and-Thinks, longs to marry Walks-with-Pumas, the handsome young son of Big Chief Blue-Lightning. But River-Song has a formidable rival in Fast-Runner, her childhood friend, who is likely to win the summer games and gain the young brave's favor.

The River People is a coming-of-age story with universal themes— love, honor, duty, tradition. But it is also an endearing portrait of the early inhabitants of a bountiful land of majestic hills, lush valleys, and the river they hold sacred. And although the author doesn't dwell on the details of Native American culture, we learn among other things that the river people live in long houses, weave clothing from cedar strips, ground acorns for flour, carve canoes from logs, and revere Father Salmon and the other spirits that watch over them. We also learn that River-Song, at age fifteen, comes late to marriage but early to the wisdom she will need, after her father passes on to that "long house in the woods," to lead the people of her village during the challenging times that lie ahead. While this is a story that will appeal to young readers, the book's themes and the cultural enrichment the book offers make it one that can be read and appreciated by readers of all ages.

Praise from readers:

The River People is a unique and refreshing story of the daily lives of the Northwestern American Indian. Partly American Indian herself, Kristen gives a vivid account of what life was probably like two hundred years ago. She incorporates love, compassion, jealousy and danger in such a way that it brings *The River People* to life and makes it a must read.

The River People provides an intriguing view inside the life of the Pacific Northwest Indians. Conflicts facing River-Song, the chief's daughter, are both culturally significant and relevant and mysterious to young people around the world in every generation.

*****

Visit
www.bookpromoting101.com
for more articles, tips and updates.

CPSIA information can be obtained at www.ICGtesting.com

228349LV00004B/285/P